Graciously Hear Us

Graciously Hear Us

General Intercessions for Cycles A, B, & C

Neil J. Draves-Arpaia

International Standard Book Number: 0-87793-657-9

Cover and text design by Brian C. Conley

Printed and bound in the United States of America.

Library of Congress Cataloging-in-Publication Data

Draves-Arpaia, Neil J.
    Graciously hear us : general intercessions for cycles A, B & C / Neil J. Draves-Arpaia.
              p.   cm.
       ISBN 0-87793-657-9
       1. General intercessions—Catholic Church.   2. Catholic Church—Liturgy—Texts. 3. Common lectionary (1992)   I. Title.
    BX2015.62.D73   1998
    264'.023—dc21

                                                    98-19810
                                                      CIP

*In memory of
my maternal grandmother,
Crestina Cappello Arpaia
(1880 - 1965),
a priestly woman who
taught me the beauty of praying for
the living and the dead.*

Contents

Solemnities and Feasts of the Lord

Holy Days

Sundays in Ordinary Time

Introduction

The *General Instruction of the Roman Missal* identifies the general intercessions (or the prayer of the faithful) as an opportunity for the people of God to exercise their priestly function by interceding for the needs of all humanity (#45). Human needs cover a wide range of concerns and issues, some of which are specifically spiritual in nature and others which are not, though they are nonetheless important to family, community, and societal life. The *Instruction* notes that it is appropriate to pray for the church, public authorities, the world's salvation, human oppression, and issues that are unique to the local community (#46).

The *Instruction* also notes that the general intercessions should be included in all celebrations where the faithful participate (#45). Interceding in prayer is a central part of Catholic worship and should not be dismissed lightly. However, composing meaningful general intercessions takes time and thoughtfulness. The more meaningful general intercessions are those that come from the people and call forth the assembly's faith, hope, and love. But it is not always possible to create fresh petitions. The general intercessions in this book are intended for pastors, liturgical planners, and presiders for Word or Communion Services who cannot always "produce from scratch" the petitions for a given liturgy. They may be used in whole or part or simply as a guide.

Graciously Hear Us seeks to respond to a wide range of spiritual and human needs. The immediate inspiration for these petitions is three-fold. First, the assigned readings of the day serve as the primary source. By using text and imagery from sacred scripture, the petitions give the assembly a better sense of "praying the word" that has just been proclaimed in light of the faith they have just professed. This helps strengthen the unity of the general intercessions to the liturgy of the word and brings it to a reverent conclusion before moving on to the liturgy of the eucharist. Second, the petitions are written in the spirit of the various liturgical seasons. And third, these petitions recognize the diversity of communities as well as universal needs and issues.

The Nature of the General Intercessions

The general intercession is a public communal prayer. Its nature is intercessory, which means that we are praying on behalf of someone or some group. As intercessors, the assembly is actively uniting itself to the mediating work of Christ, who intercedes for us at the right hand of the Power. The church, the body of Christ, is called to be a people of prayer presenting every need to God in, through, and with Christ in the power of the Holy Spirit. The Holy Spirit is also an intercessor praying through the faithful and on behalf of the faithful in the presence of God and the Lamb. The general intercessions affirm the church's Trinitarian beliefs, its Christology, pneumatology, and ecclesiology.

All prayer is the work of the Holy Spirit. As a public form of intercessory prayer, the general intercessions invite the faithful to become one voice as they present their "needs to God in every form of prayer and in petitions full of gratitude" (Phil 4:6). In most cases the First Person of the Trinity is addressed in the name of Jesus. At other times the church calls upon humankind's Redeemer, Jesus Christ. In some cases it is the Spirit who is directly invoked so that the intercessions have an epiclesis character to them. This is particularly evident during ordinary time. Some of the intercessions petition God, the Creator, or Christ to pour forth the Holy Spirit so that the church and world may abide in faith, hope, and love. Many of these petitions emphasize the Trinitarian nature of prayer and bring into bold relief the redemptive work of the Spirit. The presider's concluding prayer affirms that the church is praying in the name and spirit of Christ.

Intercessions can be a bit tricky though they appear to be a simple prayer form. All intercessions must fall under one overarching prayer: "God's will be done on earth as in heaven." Since doing and fulfilling the will of God was the heart of Jesus' life and prayer, so it must be the heart of the church's prayer. Petitions must clearly convey to the faithful that what the church is praying for at any given moment is in keeping with the heart and mind of Christ, the gospel proclamation, the truths of faith, and the church's commitment to live justly and peaceably.

The Style of the Petitions in the General Intercessions

The petitions in this book are written in various styles so as to prevent them from being overly routine and disengaging. The word "general" is not meant to suggest that the petitions should be so broad that they are ambiguous. The assembly of God's people needs to know exactly what or who they are being asked to pray for. Clarity in the general intercessions can inspire rich intercessory prayer among God's people. At the same time, clarity, as with brevity, does not mean forsaking the meaning and richness that can evoke the imagination and help raise the mind and heart to God.

There are perennial concerns that always merit prayer such as the church's growth in holiness, fidelity to the gospel, and intercession for the sick and the dead. These concerns are found in all of the intercessions either implicitly or explicitly. For Sundays in ordinary time petitions for various professions and relationships, such as educators, health care professionals, artists, parents, youth, and married and single persons, are included along with other customary petitions. Persons who are in recovery from or struggling with addictions are prayed for clearly. Issues such as sexual abuse, racial and gender discrimination, and greater openness to women's ministerial gifts in the church are also voiced in these prayers. Intercessions for the economically poor, spiritual seekers, and persecuted Christians are interspersed throughout.

At times the petitions employ the words "we," "us," and "our." It is the task of presiders and homilists to continually catechize the immediate assembly that it is praying "in union with the whole church." Over the three-year liturgical cycle it is hoped that everyone will feel that he or she has been embraced by the community in prayer.

Since the introduction (or restoration) of the general intercessions into the Roman Liturgy, the prayer of the faithful has not always been a vibrant prayer. Often petitions are so localized or personalized that they have lost their "general" character. At other times the petitions are trite and almost insignificant. And sometimes the prayer of the faithful has been limited to two or three concerns, namely the pope and bishops, the sick and the dead. The underlying message in all of this seems to be "get the petitions over with and on with the Mass." Of course, there's nothing wrong with praying for the church's leaders, the sick, or the dead. However, the ministerial priesthood is remembered in the eucharistic prayers of the church as are the faithful departed. This is not to say that the sick, the dead, or the ministerial priesthood have been eliminated in these general intercessions. To the contrary, many of the intercessions in this book pray for the church's ministers as well as the deceased. The petition on behalf of the dead allows for someone recently deceased to be remembered by name when this is pastorally sensitive and helpful for relatives or close friends who may be present and working through grief.+

The petitions in this book avoid the recent tendency to use the prayer of the faithful as a type of parish bulletin board; that is, a way of announcing things in the assembly. Rather, these petitions reflect a noticeable and intended emphasis upon

---

+ There is varied opinion as to whether or not it is appropriate to specify the deceased by name outside of a Funeral Mass or Mass for the Dead. My opinion is that the local assembly has a right to pray for those who are "dear to them," whether living or dead. Also, the liturgy belongs to the people and, therefore, the prayers should allow for their needs and concerns to be articulated whether it is for healing, for comfort, or for spiritual benefits. In the case of identifying a deceased person(s), naming is an act of remembrance and can help foster healing in those who are grieving.

fidelity to the word of God and the sacramental and spiritual life, nonviolent and compassionate living, peace, justice, environmental concerns, respect for creation, human dignity and well-being, and the church's hope of arriving at the fullness of life in the reign of God.

Leading the General Intercessions

The *General Instruction of the Roman Missal* (#47) states that the presider briefly introduces the prayer of the faithful in a way that invites the assembly into prayer. Similarly, the presider brings it to a prayerful conclusion. The petitions themselves are to be led or directed by someone other than the presider. In most circumstances this format is usually followed, though in some instances it may not be possible to have someone other than the presider offer the petitions. Since the general intercessions are a part of the liturgy of the word, the petitions are to be proclaimed from the ambo and not from the cantor's stand or some other podium.

Leading the petitions is a critical ministry as important as any other part of Catholic worship. It is imperative that the assembly understand what is being prayed for. Consequently, the effectiveness of leading the assembly in prayer requires that the proclaimer of the intercessions read *slowly, clearly,* and *directly* to the assembly. Reviewing the petitions prior to the liturgy is a *must* (especially to learn the pronunciation of people's names). Pastors and presiders should discourage other activity (e.g., the collection or the presentation of the gifts) from occurring until the general intercessions have been completed in order to foster prayerful attentiveness.

A variety of assembly prayer responses has been purposely included in the petitions. While some assemblies are accustomed to variations in the petition response, it is important for the petition leader to announce the prayer response of the day so that the assembly can learn it and repeat it.

The intercessions are meant to be prayed thoughtfully; rushing through them will only minimize the importance of the assembly's prayer. If the intercessions invite the faithful to pause for silent prayer, the petition leader should allow a meaningful pause.

The Scope of the General Intercessions

This book contains intercessions for Sunday celebrations, solemnities and holy days (in the United States), and feasts of the Lord. The number of intercessions for any given prayer of the faithful is yet another consideration. Most have been kept to six petitions although there are some with more. The purpose in including more than six is to provide liturgy planners or the presider with a few extra options. Care should be given to not unduly prolong the general intercessions.

It should be noted that some intercessions are written in litany form and can move quickly, though they should not be rushed. Ideally, litanies are to be sung. But even when this is not possible, a well done litany has the power to create a very prayerful environment. There is a beauty and a rhythm to litanies that can be culti-vated anew in the Roman Liturgy.

In some cases where the readings do not change with the cycles, e.g., Christmas, Palm Sunday, All Saints, Immaculate Conception, etc., the general intercessions are the same from year to year. Some options are provided for some of these circum-stances. For example, the Lenten intercessions have been written with the catechumenate in mind even if there are no catechumens preparing for baptism at the Easter Vigil in a given parish or other liturgical community.

Ultimately my overall concern in composing these intercessions has been the assembly of the faithful. Intercessory prayer has always enjoyed a vibrancy in the life of God's people, especially in personal prayer. May the same vibrancy be brought into the liturgical assembly so that the Spirit's gift of prayer may flourish to God's honor and glory and the spiritual good of all people.

Using the Computer Disk

The accompanying computer disk has been included to make the petitions in this book even more accessible to you. By using this disk, you will be able to re-produce the petitions to meet your particular needs.

The files on this disk are saved in either Rich Text File (rtf) or DOS Text File (txt) format, sort of "generic" formats. In order to use this disk, you must have a computer and word processing software that allows you to access it. Either a Mac-intosh or Macintosh-compatible computer or an IBM or IBM-compatible computer using a Windows operating system will be able to open the files. If you have a Macintosh computer that is several years old, it may not be able to open the disk. Once the disk is opened, most word processing programs will then be able to access the information.

When using the disk, first open "Readme.txt." This document offers further in-structions for opening the main text of *Graciously Hear Us*. When working in a Windows environment, you will need to select the option "All Files" under the "List Files of Type" heading in the dialogue box. Unless you do this, the file may not appear.

Advent Season

First Sunday of Advent (A)

Presider: Knowing the times in which we are living, let us pray that our deeds will take on the light of Christ's love.

Petition Leader: Our response is, **"Draw us to your light, O Christ."**

By the power of your Spirit inspire our hearts to learn the ways of peaceable living. We pray:

By the light of your truth open our minds to the church's teachings on justice for the economically poor among us. We pray:

By the voices of the prophets, past and present, guide us away from violence in our ordinary actions and speech. We pray:

By our hope in your coming in glory strengthen our resolve to live honorably and respectfully whether at work or at play. We pray:

By the love you manifest in the eucharist help us to be more genuinely concerned for the moral and spiritual good of our children, the elderly, and the sick among us. We pray:

By the splendor of your mercy welcome into the day of salvation those who have died (especially _____).
We pray:

Presider: Eternal God, graciously receive the prayers of your church that joyfully awaits the coming of Christ, who lives and reigns forever.

First Sunday of Advent (B)

Presider: Let us pray to be mindful of God's ways as we await the coming of Christ.

Petition Leader: Our response today is, **"Saving God, help us."**

Remembering God's faithfulness toward the House of Israel, we pray for the grace to be faithful to God's will in our lives. As we await the day of Christ Jesus, we ask:

Mindful of Christ's teaching to keep vigilant, we ask the Spirit to intensify our life of prayer. As we await the day of Christ Jesus, we ask:

Acknowledging our need for God's redeeming love, we pray that Christ will find us ready for the reign of heaven. As we await the day of Christ Jesus, we ask:

Longing for God to open the heavens and come down, we ask for the grace to open our hearts to let in the poor of Christ. As we await the day of Christ Jesus, we ask:

Grateful for the many spiritual gifts we possess, we pray that Christ will find us working diligently for the final harvest of justice and peace. As we await the day of Christ Jesus, we ask:

Rejoicing that God is the potter and we the clay, we ask for the grace to receive the word of God that fashions us into a holy priesthood, a nation dedicated to right. As we await the day of Christ Jesus, we ask:

Presider: God our Creator, fill us with the new life of grace that we may cling to your love and abide in hope as the day of Christ draws near. Grant our prayers in Jesus' name.

First Sunday of Advent (C)

Presider: Let us pray to conduct ourselves in ways that are pleasing to God.

Petition Leader: Our common prayer response is: **"Christ, our Justice, hear our prayer."**

Through the grace and peace of your Holy Spirit strengthen us in our commitment to live peaceably with one another. We pray:

Through the word of your prophets and apostles open our hearts to receive the teachings of the church calling us to greater justice. We pray:

Through the example of our blameless conduct may we raise up our youth to be Christian adults overflowing with love for God and neighbor. We pray:

Through our dedication to honorable and respectful living help us to build cities where all dwell securely, particularly the economically poor. We pray:

Through the signs of our times teach us to discern your presence calling us to live more reverently. We pray:

Through the gift of the eucharist may we draw hope in your abiding kindness when we fail in the requirements of justice and compassion. We pray:

Through the constancy of your love receive with tenderness the dead who appear before you in the humility of their lives (especially _____). We pray:

Presider: Merciful God, fulfiller of promises, receive our prayers through Jesus Christ, who is our justice with you, now and forever.

Second Sunday of Advent (A)

Presider: Let us pray in joyful hope as we await the coming of Christ.

Petition Leader: Our response is, **"Promise of Ages, hear our prayer."**

As the church strives to discern the signs of our times, may it be consoled by the Spirit's gifts of wisdom and knowledge. We pray in joyful hope:

As we make pilgrimage through a culture often hostile to the gift of human life, may Christians be courageous in their witness to gospel truths. We pray in joyful hope:

As the world struggles to regain its spiritual moorings, may the teachings of the church provide a straight path to the mystery of God in Christ. We pray in joyful hope:

As we raise our voice in prayer for God's kingdom, may we prepare for the reign of love by cultivating a harvest of justice. We pray in joyful hope:

As we dream of a new heaven and a new earth, may we be sustained by Christ's promise of a new creation more glorious than the first. We pray in joyful hope:

Presider: God, receive the prayers of your church and draw us all to Christ, whom we long for with joy. We pray in Jesus' name.

Second Sunday of Advent (B)

Presider: As we wait for the new creation, let us pray to be filled with the love and peace of Christ.

Petition Leader: Our prayer response is, **"Consoling Spirit, be with us."**

For the church, that it may courageously herald the liberating love of God to those held down by sin. While awaiting the new creation, we pray:

For all who promote healing through spiritual counseling, medical arts, and behavioral sciences, that they may help others find peaceful pathways to the future. While awaiting the new creation, we pray:

For those who call the world to conversion by setting aside greed and violence, that their voices will rouse all peoples to seek peace. While awaiting the new creation, we pray:

For funeral directors, grief counselors, pastoral ministers, and therapists in their ministry to the grieving, that they may be instruments of God's comfort and care. While awaiting the new creation, we pray:

For our children as they look forward to Christmas, that they may come to recognize that Christ alone is the greatest gift. While awaiting the new creation, we pray:

For Christian parents and grandparents, that they may be prudent in their gift-giving and avoid wasteful spending. While awaiting the new creation, we pray:

Presider: God, you call us to set our hearts on the lasting joys of the new creation. May your consoling Spirit guide us in right paths until all is ready for Christ, our Savior.

Second Sunday of Advent (C)

Presider: God's mercy and justice accompany us through life. With a confident faith, let us pray.

Petition Leader: Our response is: **"Loving God, hear us."**

Through our faith in Christ, the Dawn of Justice, gather us into a community of praise and compassionate service. With Advent longing, we ask:

Through the consoling love of the Spirit remove from the sick and dying the robe of misery and mourning. With Advent longing, we ask:

Through the voices of prophets, past and present, lead back to you those misled by the false promises of a drug and commercial culture. With Advent longing, we ask:

Through our commitment to gospel values at home, in schools, and in the workplace, enable youth to choose lifestyles of blameless conduct. With Advent longing, we ask:

Through the wisdom of the Spirit give our legislators the courage to pursue the requirements of justice for the most needy and vulnerable. With Advent longing, we ask:

Through the power of the eternal name of Christ bring to new life all who have died (particularly _____). With Advent longing, we ask:

Presider: Sustaining God, receive our prayers and bring to fulfillment the good you have begun in us. May we be found rejoicing on the day of Christ Jesus, who lives and reigns forever and ever.

Third Sunday of Advent (A)

Presider: Let us pray with hearts that long for God's reign.

Petition Leader: Our response is, **"Christ Jesus, hear our prayer."**

Christ came to free humanity from its slavery to death; may the Savior's return find the church laboring to safeguard all life. As we await the new creation, we pray:

Christ opened a straight path to God's compassion for the sinner; may the faith and love of Christians inspire others to seek God's mercy. As we await the new creation, we pray:

Christ transformed the landscape of human suffering; may the church's pastoral ministries continue the healing work of the Messiah. As we await the new creation, we pray:

Christ, the Promise of Ages, sent the Spirit into the world to lead all to the truth; may the Spirit guide those searching for God. As we await the new creation, we pray:

Christ affirmed that it is not on bread alone that we live; may we strive to live moderately and consume less. As we await the new creation, we pray:

Christ will come as the just judge of the living and the dead; may all who have died in Christ be crowned with everlasting joy, (especially _____). As we await the new creation, we pray:

Presider: God, hear our prayers and uphold us in faith until all is ready to receive the Dawn of Justice, who is Christ, the Lord.

Third Sunday of Advent (B)

Presider: God, who is the joy of our souls, brings us to perfection through Christ and the Spirit. Let us pray that all will be sustained by God's redeeming love until the Dawn of Justice breaks upon creation.

Petition Leader: Our prayer response is, **"God of peace, uphold your servants."**

Like Israel that hoped for the promised messiah may the world center its hope on God's promise to make all things new in Christ. As we await the Dawn of Justice, we pray:

Like John the Baptist may the church witness to the light of Christ that leads to enduring peace. As we await the Dawn of Justice, we pray:

Like Mary, the favored daughter of Israel, may we praise God's ageless mercy that fills the hungry with good things. As we await the Dawn of Justice, we pray:

Like Christ, God's Anointed, may all Christians live in fidelity to the Spirit who clothes God's people in grace. As we await the Dawn of Justice, we pray:

Like Paul, the apostle, may we trust the Spirit to preserve the church in unity and love. As we await the Dawn of Justice, we pray:

Like the prophets and saints throughout the ages may we, too, draw new life and health through the gift of persevering prayer. As we await the Dawn of Justice, we pray:

Presider: Redeeming God, hear our prayers. May your Spirit prepare us to receive the mantle of mercy that Christ will bestow on those who have trusted your power to save. We ask this in the name of Jesus, whose coming we await.

Third Sunday of Advent (C)

Presider: Let us ask God to pour the Spirit of love into our hearts as we prepare for the coming of Christ.

Petition Leader: Let us call out in faith: **"Spirit of Jesus, fill us!"**

Spirit of Jesus, guard our hearts and minds from all selfishness and greed, especially as we prepare for Christmas. We pray:

Spirit of Jesus, turn any discouragement in us into a confident faith in God's saving power. We pray:

Spirit of Jesus, renew in us a firm dedication to work for greater peace in our families, our personal relationships, and our society. We pray:

Spirit of Jesus, help us to abandon behaviors that intimidate and humiliate others. We pray:

Spirit of Jesus, remove all fear and anxiety from the hearts of those who are seriously ill and dying. We pray:

Spirit of Jesus, raise up our beloved dead that they may exult with joy in the city of God (especially _____). We pray:

Presider: Spirit of wisdom and peace, guide us by the light of God's word. Fill us with gratitude and trust, and prepare us to receive Christ, who lives and reigns forever.

Fourth Sunday of Advent (A)

Presider: Sisters and brothers, the day draws near. Let us intensify our prayers to be a faith-filled people longing for the Dawn of Joy.

Petition Leader: Our prayer response is, **"Christ, hear our prayer."**

Christ descended from David's line and assumed our humanity. May the world grow in its respect for all that is genuinely human. With hope-filled joy, we ask:

Paul, the apostle, sent greetings of peace to the church of Rome. May the Catholic church proclaim the peace of Christ through the apostolic ministry of Pope [*name*] and the bishops of the world. With hope-filled joy, we ask:

Christ was conceived through the power of the Holy Spirit. May the begetting Spirit guide the church to the fullness of the mystery of Christ. With hope-filled joy, we ask:

Joseph received Mary, the Christ-bearer, into his home. May we receive others, regardless of race or creed, as bearers of the mystery of God. With hope-filled joy, we ask:

Joseph responded in faith to the revelation he received. May people of goodwill be more alert to the Spirit's prompting and respond with a trusting faith. With hope-filled joy, we ask:

Christ is the promise foretold by the prophets. When Christ comes may the dead inherit all that has been promised. (In particular we remember _____ .) With hope-filled joy, we ask:

Presider: God and Abba of Jesus, you sent your Word to dwell among us. Hear our prayers, for we long for the fullness of life that Christ will bring. We pray in Jesus' name.

Fourth Sunday of Advent (B)

Presider: Like David, the ruler of Israel, and Mary, the Mother of Jesus, let us praise the favors of God in a spirit of hope-filled joy.

Petition Leader: Our prayer response is, **"God of mercy, fill us with hope."**

You have established your reign of love in Christ, our Emmanuel. May your church abide in the Spirit of Christ. As we watch for the Radiant Dawn, we pray:

Christ came among us and proclaimed your loving kindness. Strengthen Pope [*name*], the church's bishops, and clergy that they may fulfill their ministry in a spirit of mercy. As we watch for the Radiant Dawn, we pray:

Through Mary we have received the promised Messiah. Through our fidelity to your will may the world continue to experience your saving power. As we watch for the Radiant Dawn, we pray:

By the word of the prophets, Israel was filled with hope. By our prophetic witness to the sanctity of life may the most vulnerable of society be strengthened. As we watch for the Radiant Dawn, we pray:

In Christ your covenant of love endures forever. Watch over all who live in the covenant of marriage that their love may be life-giving. As we watch for the Radiant Dawn, we pray:

Your Anointed took up our humanity to lead us to the reign of peace. May the dead who took up Christ's life through faith find kind welcome in heaven (especially _____). As we watch for the Radiant Dawn, we pray:

Presider: Loving God, as we wait for the Dawn of Salvation, sustain us in hope and guide our feet into the pathways of peace. We pray in the name and Spirit of Jesus, our Emmanuel and your Beloved.

Fourth Sunday of Advent (C)

Presider: Jesus fulfilled the will of God by coming among us in the power of the Holy Spirit. Let us pray that Christ's sacramental presence will enable us to live the spiritual mysteries we hold by faith.

Petition Leader: With Advent longing let us call out: **"Rouse your power and come, Christ Jesus!"**

Come in the power of God's creative love to guide the leaders of our church and world into the ways of universal peace. We pray:

Come in the power of compassion that love may be the rule of our lives. We pray:

Come in the power of justice that we might be a fit dwelling place for you in the Spirit. We pray:

Come in the power of the Holy Spirit that we may be stirred to praise your glory at this holy table. We pray:

Come in the power of humility that we may learn how to be more self-giving and less demanding. We pray:

Come in the power of your resurrection for all the dead who trusted your saving Word (especially _____). We pray:

Presider: Come Jesus, Savior and Redeemer, in the power of your Holy Spirit that we may have new life in your name. May your life shine forth in us now and forever.

Christmas Season

Midnight Mass or Christmas Day (A, B, and C)

Option #1

Presider: On this holy night (day) let us implore the God of perfect peace to fill us with the glory of the Word-Made-Flesh.

Petition Leader: In our joy let us call out: **"Fill us with peace, saving God."**

You have given us Christ to be our light. In the name of the Prince of Peace, enable us to be a people ever eager to do what is right, peaceable, and just. We pray:

You have given us Christ, the Living Word. In the name of the Wonder-Counselor, pour out the Spirit of wisdom and understanding on all religious leaders. We pray:

You have given us Christ to be the herald of good news to the poor and lowly. In the name of the Anointed One, help the church as it carries on Christ's mission of mercy. We pray:

You have given us Christ to redeem humanity from the forces of death. In the name of Emmanuel, teach us to set aside any jealousy and animosity that deprive us of intimacy with you. We pray:

You have given us the descendant of David to be our blessed hope. In the name of the risen Savior, comfort all who mourn with your tender compassion. We pray:

You have given us a vision of your glory in the birth of Christ. In the name of Jesus, the child of Mary, bring all the dead to the reign of eternal light and life (especially _____). We pray:

Presider: God of glory, the light of Christ reveals your love for us. Receive our prayers and grant that we may always receive your Word-Made-Flesh with grateful hearts. We ask this in Jesus' name.

Christmas Day or Midnight Mass (A, B, and C)

Option #2

Presider: In Christ the goodness of God has appeared in our midst. Let us pray to be open to the gift of God's saving love.

Petition Leader: With joyful hearts we ask: **"God of glory, hear our prayer!"**

Inspire church leaders through the Holy Spirit of unity to bring all Christians together in common praise of Jesus Christ. We pray:

Fill the heads of households with the gift of wisdom so that they may guide their children to the redeeming light of Christ. We pray:

Sustain the economically poor, the sick, and the lonely through our efforts to provide them with quality care. We pray:

Enlighten us by the gospel of salvation that we may reject godless ways of excessive spending and wastefulness of our earth's resources. We pray:

Cleanse us by the gift of the eucharist that we may image Christ, the Word-Made-Flesh, to persons of other faith traditions. We pray:

Through the saving mystery of Jesus Christ, may the dead find the fullness of life (especially _____). We pray:

Presider: Gracious God, with the birth of Christ, your glory has shown among us. Strengthen us to enflesh your love that brings life to all people. Grant our prayers in the name of our Savior, Jesus Christ.

Midnight Mass or Solemn Liturgy During the Day (A, B, and C)—Litany Form+

Option #3

Presider: Through the birth of Jesus the glory of God has shown around us. Let us pray to be filled with the Savior's peace.

Petition Leader: Our response to each invocation is: **"May your peace be with us."**

By your coming among us, O Christ . . .

By your power as God, O Christ . . .

By the love you manifested in the flesh, O Christ . . .

Through the beauty of your humanity, O Christ . . .

Through your humble birth, O Christ . . .

Through the truth of your word, O Christ . . .

Through your life-giving death and resurrection, O Christ . . .

Through the power of your Holy Spirit, O Christ . . .

For all who profess you as Light from Light, O Christ . . .

For all who acclaim your everlasting glory, O Christ . . .

For all who are baptized by water and the Spirit, O Christ . . .

For all who announce your gospel of peace, O Christ . . .

For all who are fed at your table this day, O Christ . . .

For all who have died in your peace, O Christ . . .

Presider: O Christ, you are the splendor of God. Bless the people who invoke your love and continue to sustain us in your kindness and fidelity, for you live and reign forever and ever.

+ As with any litany, these invocations should be proclaimed boldly and swiftly, but not in a rushed or hurried manner. For this reason the litany extends beyond the customary number of intercessions.

Christmas Vigil or Christmas Day Masses for Children (A, B, and C)

Presider: Jesus is the Son of God who teaches us how to live as God's children. On this special day we pray to live as Jesus taught.

Petition Leader: Our response to each petition is, **"Jesus, we pray to you."**

Jesus, you were sent by God to bring us peace. May we practice kindness in our families and with our friends. As we celebrate your birth, we say:

Jesus, you chose to live as one of us. May we choose to live like you by loving God and neighbor. As we celebrate your birth, we say:

Jesus, you are God's gift to us. May we be a gift to you by obeying your commandments. As we celebrate your birth, we say:

Jesus, the angels sang your praises when you came into the world. May we sing your praises in our daily prayers. As we celebrate your birth, we say:

Jesus, the poor shepherds came to pay you honor. May we show our care for people who are poor by sharing our food and clothing. As we celebrate your birth, we say:

Jesus, you give your love to people of every race, language, and age. May we show respect to all the people you lived and died for. As we celebrate your birth, we say:

Presider: Loving God, our hearts are happy at the birth of Jesus. Grant that we may all live as your sons and daughters, and hear our prayers in Jesus' name.

Holy Family (A, B, and C)

Presider: The love of God has burst forth in the coming of Christ. Let us pray that the church, a family of faith, will abide in love.

Petition Leader: Our response is, **"Receive our prayers, O God."**

That our worship of God and celebration of the Savior's birth will deepen our bonds of unity as brothers and sisters in faith, we pray:

That the humanity of Jesus will help us to value the human dignity of every person, we pray:

That the mutual love of husband and wife will be a source of security and blessing for their children, we pray:

That adult children will clothe their elderly parents with kindness, respect, and care, we pray:

That respect for parents will take root in young children, we pray:

That family harmony will be safeguarded through each member's willingness to be an instrument of peace and goodwill, we pray:

That the dead who have acclaimed Christ as God's revealing light will be found praising God in the heavenly temple (particularly _____), we pray:

Presider: God of enduring kindness, hear our prayers. In Christ you call us to be a family of faith. May each household be enriched in wisdom and love and know your help in time of trial. Grant our prayers through your Word-Made-Flesh, Jesus Christ.

Mary, Mother of God (A, B, and C)

Presider: On this first day of the new year, let us implore God's blessings and protection, assured of Mary's intercession.

Petition Leader: Let us invoke the Savior's name after each petition, saying: **"Jesus, Son of Mary, hear us!"**

We pray to be blessed with a love for God's word. May our knowledge of sacred scripture guide us in the ways of Christ. In joyful hope we ask:

We implore the blessing of nonviolent living wherever there is open hostility. May each nation, each household, each individual be freed from the slavery of hatred and dissension. In joyful hope we ask:

We pray for the blessing of good health. May our resolve to live healthier and holier lives be sustained by the Holy Spirit's wisdom and guidance. In joyful hope we ask:

We ask to be blessed with the gift of laughter. May joy, the fruit of the Spirit's work, make every home a place of happiness and relaxation. In joyful hope we ask:

We implore God's blessing upon the most vulnerable among us. May God protect the elderly, our children, the developmentally and physically disabled, and the homeless. In joyful hope we ask:

We ask God's blessing upon all who will assume a public office today. May local and state leaders across the nation be blessed with right judgment and undertake their duties with moral integrity. In joyful hope we ask:

We ask God to bless us with every spiritual gift that, like Mary, we may place our lives in service of the gospel of peace. In joyful hope we ask:

Presider: God of love and joy, you desire our complete happiness. May we, like Mary, find that happiness in your blessings. We ask this in Jesus' name.

Second Sunday After Christmas (A, B, and C)

Presider: Christ is the wisdom of God made manifest. Let us summon the Spirit of God to fill us with the wisdom and love of Christ.

Petition Leader: Our response is, **"Wisdom of God, be with us."**

Guide church leaders, all ordained, pastoral, and lay ministers. May the spiritual blessings God has given them help build up the body of Christ, the church. We pray:

Safeguard all the faithful. May all who have been chosen by God to be adopted sons and daughters in Christ be filled with the gift of love. We pray:

Enlighten us by means of truth. May all who are in periods of discernment, especially those considering vocations, be guided by the Spirit. We pray:

Help all spiritual seekers who desire to know the one true God. May the Savior's Spirit give each person insight on their journey in faith. We pray:

Bring to the fullness of life all who have died praising the glory of God. May the dead find rest in the Christ (particularly _____). We pray:

Presider: How glorious is your name through all the earth, loving God! You have chosen to dwell among us in Word and Spirit. May all praise your name and be enlightened through your gifts of faith, hope, and love, through Christ our Savior.

Epiphany (A, B, and C)

Option #1

Presider: All humanity is drawn to God through the light of Christ. Let us pray that our spiritual gifts will enable us to reach the fullness of light and life.

Petition Leader: Our prayer response is, **"Draw us to yourself, Living Word."**

Through the light of faith inspire us to seek you continuously in the ordinary and common places. We ask in faith:

Through the light of wisdom show us the path that leads to healthier lifestyles and spiritual maturity. We ask in faith:

Through the light of hope renew our strength in time of illness, grief, and personal trial. We ask in faith:

Through the light of truth enable national leaders to see new horizons for universal peace. We ask in faith:

Through the light of justice help us as a society to share our material gifts with those less fortunate. We ask in faith:

Through the light of love transform any ill will and hostility in us into forgiveness and kindness. We ask in faith:

Through the light of everlasting peace scatter the darkness of death for those whose earthly journey has ended (particularly _____). We ask in faith:

Presider: God of everlasting glory, you have revealed Christ to be the light to the nations. Receive our prayers through Christ, who manifests your love for us eternally.

Epiphany (A, B, and C)

Option #2

Presider: All nations shall come to adore the Light of Love who is Jesus Christ. Through our intercessory prayers, let us ask that the light of Christ shine more brightly in our world.

Petition Leader: Our response is, **"Christ, our Light, hear our prayer!"**

For the church, that it will continuously place its spiritual gifts in loving service of God and God's people. We pray:

For all who open their hearts in worship of Christ at this eucharistic table; may our communion in the body and blood of Christ enable the gospel to be enfleshed in us. We pray:

For those who search for God in nature; may its wonders draw them to the Word-Made-Flesh, through whom all things were made. We pray:

For any who seek to do violence to newborn life; may the Light of Truth dispel the darkness of minds and hearts closed to the gospel of life. We pray:

For those who are unable to trust that Jesus Christ is the light of redeeming love; may the transforming grace of the Spirit overcome all obstacles to true faith. We pray:

For those who walked by the light of faith in the risen Jesus and have completed their earthly pilgrimage (especially _____); may the glory of Christ shine upon them forever. We pray:

Presider: God of compassion, graciously hear our prayers and help us to follow the way of love that leads to everlasting life. Grant this through Christ, our Lord.

Epiphany (A, B, and C)

Option #3

Presider: Rejoicing that the light of God's love shines among us, let us pray united in the one Spirit.

Petition Leader: Our response today is, **"Savior of all, hear us."**

We worship you as Light from Light. Draw us to yourself by the light of your Word and Spirit. As we rejoice in your birth, we pray:

We sing your praise, Savior of the nations. Unite all believers in a common household of faith. As we rejoice in your birth, we pray:

We give you thanks, Redeemer of the world. May our gratitude show itself in our respect for the gift of life. As we rejoice in your birth, we pray:

We proclaim you as the Word-Made-Flesh. By the truth of your Word, lead us away from evil. As we rejoice in your birth, we pray:

We celebrate your dying and rising in this meal. May the Spirit deepen our bonds of love with all who are yours, regardless of race, language, or way of life. As we rejoice in your birth, we pray:

We profess that you alone are the Holy One. May the Spirit help the world to believe that you are the way to everlasting peace. As we rejoice in your birth, we pray:

Presider: God of glory, you have sent Christ into the world to lead us to the splendor of the New Jerusalem. Receive our praises and strengthen the faith that unites us in the mystery of Christ, who lives and reigns with you and the Holy Spirit, one God, forever and ever.

Baptism of the Lord (A)

Presider: In our baptism Christ grasps us by the hand and calls the church to carry on his mission of mercy. Let us invoke the Spirit of Jesus to help us.

Petition Leader: In the light of faith let us call out: **"Light of Nations, pour forth your Spirit!"**

Upon the church as it calls nations to assure the victory of justice for the poor, the oppressed, the unborn, and the terminally ill, we pray:

Upon our parish communities as we welcome the newly baptized, new neighbors, and new citizens, we pray:

Upon the sick and all who are in periods of physical and emotional recovery, we pray:

Upon this assembly gathered in faith to be fed the Living Word of compassion, we pray:

Upon all who struggle to fulfill the demands of God in the face of hostility toward religion, we pray:

Upon those who are unable to recognize Christ as God's Anointed, we pray:

Upon the dead who have hoped in the resurrection of the just (particularly _____), we pray:

Presider: Redeeming God, may your favor come to rest on us through your Spirit. Enable your people to remain faithful to the mission of Jesus, through whom we invoke your blessings now and forever.

Baptism of the Lord (B)

Presider: Anointed in the Spirit, Jesus brought God's healing love to our world. As we bring our Christmas season to a close, let us pray that Christ, the Light of Nations, will sustain us in faith, hope, and love.

Petition Leader: Our prayer response is, **"Light of Nations, be with us."**

As we call for the victory of justice and compassion for the less fortunate and economically poor among us, we pray:

As we continue to break every form of captivity that keeps humanity locked in racism, sexism, and the darkness of death, we pray:

As we strive to make the church a place of welcome and warmth for all people who have been baptized in Christ, we pray:

As we herald the gospel of healing in the midst of conflict and division, we pray:

As we use our spiritual gifts and collective wisdom to sustain the sick and to find cures for disease, we pray:

As we renew our baptismal covenant with Christ through word and sacrament at this eucharistic table, we pray:

As we call upon God's mercy to rest upon those whose earthly pilgrimage has been completed (especially _____), we pray:

Presider: Creating God, as your favor came to rest upon Jesus in the waters of the Jordan, his saving mission began. May Christ's mission of mercy be extended through the church until your loving designs are fulfilled. Grant our prayer through your Anointed and our Savior, Jesus Christ.

Baptism of the Lord (C)

Presider: Full of anticipation in receiving God's mercy and favor, let us pray that the anointing Spirit will keep the light of Christ kindled in us.

Petition Leader: Our prayer response today is: **"Beloved of God, hear our prayer."**

May the Spirit of God kindle in our hearts the fire of compassion that our works of mercy may bring comfort to the imprisoned, the dying, and the hungry. We pray:

May the Spirit of God kindle in all Christians the fire of unity that God's praises may be sung in the light of one faith, one baptism, at one holy table. We pray:

May the Spirit of God kindle in us the fire of peace that we may work to overcome grievances with forgiveness. We pray:

May the Spirit of God kindle in us the fire of justice that Christ's liberating light may extend to all oppressed by greed and selfishness. We pray:

May the Spirit of God kindle in us the fire of persevering prayer that we may experience God's grace and favor daily. We pray:

May the Spirit of God kindle in us the fire of hope that we may be consoled at the death of those we love (especially _____). We pray:

Presider: God of everlasting glory, in Jesus, your Beloved, all the families of the earth find blessing. Receive our prayers and keep your Spirit alive in us. We ask this in the name of Jesus, upon whom your favor rests.

Lenten Season

Ash Wednesday (A, B, and C)

Option #1

Presider: We have marked ourselves for our Lenten journey. Let us pray to be more faithful to the gospel and arrive at Easter joy.

Petition Leader: Our prayer response is, **"Renew your life in us, O God."**

Help us to be more alert to the voice of Christ appealing to us through the cries of the poor. We pray:

Help us to alter our lifestyles when we consume more than what we really need. We pray:

Help us to discard any religious displays that are insincere. We pray:

Help us to cultivate a richer prayer life centered in your Word. We pray:

Help us to fast from harshness and arrogance in our actions. We pray:

Help us to build bridges between enemies. We pray:

Help us to show others your compassion that we may be received with compassion. We pray:

Presider: God, our help and strength, by the grace of your Spirit enable us to live in greater fidelity to the gospel of reconciliation and rejoice in the peace it offers. Grant this through Christ, our Lord.

Ash Wednesday (A, B, and C)

Option #2

Presider: Let us pray that our Lenten repentance will enable us to be more compassionate.

Petition Leader: Our prayer response is, **"Lord, may we be merciful."**

Help us to consume less so as to feed the hungry more often. We pray:

Stir us to reach out to the unwanted and unloved and provide them a home in our hearts. We pray:

Enable us to comfort those imprisoned or confined by fear and loneliness. We pray:

Help us to be present to others in their sorrow. We pray:

Give us courage to speak out against violence and injustice. We pray:

Free us to let go of grudges and strive for forgiveness. We pray:

Bless us with the gift of prayer to seek your grace for the living and dead. We pray:

Presider: God, grace our lives with your mercy that we may be merciful and follow the way of Christ, who loved us even to his death. We ask for your help through Christ, our Redeemer.

Ash Wednesday (A, B, and C)

Option #3

Presider: Having begun our Lenten journey, let us ask for the grace of genuine repentance.

Petition Leader: Our response is: **"Renew us in your mercy, O God."**

Strengthen our resolve to live more patiently with others' imperfections. We pray:

Help us to bear wrongs courageously and not return evil for evil. We pray:

Open our eyes to recognize the many opportunities for being a healing presence at home and in the workplace. We pray:

Deepen in us the gift of persevering prayer especially in times of doubt and discouragement. We pray:

Inspire in us a desire to act more compassionately toward those who are less fortunate. We pray:

Empower us to be rich in kindness and less harsh in our speech and judgments of others. We pray:

Help us to overcome our petty jealousies, greediness, and indifference to the plight of the poor. We pray:

Enable each of us to invest ourselves in living justly, unimpeded by any arrogance, false pride, and racism within us. We pray:

Presider: Merciful God, your gospel of peace calls us to pursue the way of love. May this Lenten season be rich in spiritual blessings as we strive to follow Christ, in whose name we ask for your mercy.

First Sunday of Lent (A)

Presider: Our belief in the resurrection of Jesus is a gift of faith. Let us nurture it with prayer as we call upon the Holy Spirit to help us in our Lenten journey.

Petition Leader: Our response is, **"Grace our lives, O Holy Spirit."**

May we come to rely on the Holy Spirit to lead us to places where God can speak to us in the intimacy of prayer. We pray:

May the example of Christ in the desert be a source of strength whenever we are tempted to disbelieve the word of God. We pray:

May the Holy Spirit enlighten the hearts and minds of those preparing for baptism and reception into the Catholic church. We pray:

May the Spirit of justice not allow any desire for personal prosperity to lure us away from loving God above all else. We pray:

May the Spirit of truth teach us obedience to God's will that all creation may live in harmony and peace. We pray:

May the Spirit of Jesus bestow the overflowing gift of risen life upon the dead (particularly _____). We pray:

Presider: Compassionate God, the obedience of Jesus raised a fallen world. Sustain us by your Spirit that we may live in fidelity to your Word. Grant our prayer through Christ, your servant and our Savior.

First Sunday of Lent (B)

Presider: Since the time of fulfillment has begun in Christ, let us pray to be renewed in the covenant of mercy that leads to everlasting life.

Petition Leader: Our prayer response is, **"Renew us in your love."**

Creating God, you promised Noah that the earth would live in the security of your love. Help us to care for the earth and make it a place of security for all peoples. We ask for your mercy and pray:

Redeeming Word, you call the world to live in God's peace. Help us reform our lives according to the gospel of life. We ask for your mercy and pray:

Indwelling Spirit, you come as a gift to lead all people to the fountain of salvation. Guide those who are preparing for baptism. We ask for your mercy and pray:

Sustaining God, you uphold those who walk humbly in your presence. May your Word and Spirit purify the church of all arrogance and pride. We ask for your mercy and pray:

Merciful God, Christ brought your liberating love to all things in heaven and earth. May our actions safeguard human freedom and rights. We ask for your mercy and pray:

Gracious God, in the waters of life we have promised to live as your holy people. Strengthen us in grace that we may live reverently and compassionately. We ask for your mercy and pray:

Presider: God, Trinity of love, hear our prayers to be renewed in spirit. May our Lenten journey bring us to the joys of Easter. We pray in Jesus' name.

First Sunday of Lent (C)

Presider: Our belief in the resurrection of Jesus is a gift of faith. Let us nurture it with prayer as we call upon the Holy Spirit to help us in our Lenten journey.

Petition Leader: Our response is, **"Grace our lives, O Holy Spirit."**

May we come to rely on the Holy Spirit to lead us to places where God can speak to us in the intimacy of prayer. We pray:

May the example of Christ in the desert be a source of strength whenever we are tempted to disbelieve the word of God. We pray:

May God's freeing love empower us to place our best material and spiritual gifts at the disposal of the Holy Spirit for the common good. We pray:

May any spiritual mediocrity in us be replaced by a desire to live the paschal mystery of Jesus in our everyday actions. We pray:

May those who are preparing for baptism and reception into the Catholic church be guided by the Spirit of wisdom and peace. We pray:

May we courageously witness to Jesus Christ through faith-inspired works of peace, justice, love, and compassion. We pray:

May those who called upon the name of Jesus in faith during their earthly journey hear the voice of Christ welcoming them into the joy of heaven (especially _____). We pray:

Presider: Saving God, through the Spirit you led Jesus into the desert to prepare him for his mission of mercy. Lead us by the same Spirit during this Lenten season that we may be spiritually prepared to celebrate the resurrection. We pray in the name of Jesus, who lives and reigns with you and the Holy Spirit, one God forever and ever.

Second Sunday of Lent (A)

Presider: Sisters and brothers, our covenant with God in Christ brings us the gift of salvation. In the name of God's Chosen One let us raise our voices in prayer.

Petition Leader: Our response is: **"Saving God, hear our prayer."**

In the saving mission of Christ, the Law and the prophets are perfectly fulfilled. May the church provide our world with a prophetic witness to love and peace. We pray:

On Tabor the face of Jesus changed in prayer. Through our prayers of repentance may our lives be changed to more perfectly image Christ. We pray:

You called Abram to leave the security of his homeland. May we trust your grace to sustain us as we leave behind the ways of sin and death. We pray:

You instructed the apostles to listen to Jesus. May we follow their example and take to heart the gospel's call to be compassionate and forgiving. We pray:

Jesus ascended Calvary out of love for the world. Help us to endure patiently any opposition we encounter in proclaiming the sanctity of life. We pray:

By his cross Jesus robbed death of its power. May the power of the cross bring eternal life to those who have died (especially _____). We pray:

Presider: God in heaven, Jesus taught us to pray in his name, for he is your Beloved. Fulfill in us your saving will, and by the Spirit's gift of prayer sustain us in Christ, our Lord.

Second Sunday of Lent (B)

Presider: Sisters and brothers, our covenant with God in Christ brings new life. In the name of God's Beloved, let us pray for the life of the world.

Petition Leader: Our prayer response today is, **"Saving God, hear us."**

In the saving mission of Christ, the Law and the prophets are perfectly fulfilled. Enrich the church with your Spirit that Christ's mission of mercy may flourish in every age. In Jesus' name we ask:

On the holy mountain the disciples were called to listen to Jesus. May those who are approaching baptism be filled with a love for the gospel of Christ. In Jesus' name we ask:

God promised Abraham descendants more numerous than the stars. May we not withhold ourselves from the gospel that promises endless life. In Jesus' name we ask:

Christ endured the cross so as to reveal God's great love. May all who carry the cross of suffering be given every grace and consolation. In Jesus' name we ask:

Nothing separates us from God except our failure to love in accord with God's will. Help love to abound more and more in every human heart. In Jesus' name we ask:

Presider: God, ever rich in mercy, grant that the love of Christ may dwell in us and that our prayers be acceptable to you. We ask this in the name of Jesus, our intercessor with you.

Second Sunday of Lent (C)

Presider: Sisters and brothers, our covenant with God in Christ is the cause of our hope. In the name of God's Chosen One let us raise our voices in prayer.

Petition Leader: Our response is, **"Sustaining God, hear us!"**

You called Abram to trust your word. Increase our faith and trust in your Word of Redemption, Jesus Christ. We pray:

In the saving mission of Christ, the Law and the prophets are perfectly fulfilled. Strengthen us in our resolve to pursue the law of love as Jesus taught. We pray:

On Tabor the face of Jesus changed in prayer. Through our prayers of repentance may our lives be changed to more perfectly image your Chosen Servant. We pray:

The apostles were instructed to listen to Jesus. May we follow their example and take to heart the gospel's call to be compassionate toward those who suffer. We pray:

Jesus ascended Calvary out of love for the sinful. Give us strength to endure the struggles necessary to establish greater peace upon the earth. We pray:

Through the teaching of the apostles the faithful were eager for the coming of Christ. Deepen our hope that in Christ the dead receive a share in his glory. (In particular we ask that eternal life be given to _____ .) We pray:

Presider: God in heaven, Jesus taught us to pray in his name, for he is your Beloved. Fulfill in us your saving will, and by the Spirit's gift of prayer sustain us in Christ, our Lord.

Third Sunday of Lent (A)

Presider: Jesus is God's gift to us that we might draw abundant life from the fountain of salvation. In our thirst for God's life-giving grace and peace, we turn to Christ for help.

Petition Leader: Our prayer response is: **"Christ, be merciful."**

When discouragement and frustration mark our days and we grumble in our discontent, show us your kindness. We pray:

When we hear your gospel of peace calling us but our hearts have been hardened by violence, indifference, and careless living, show us your love. We pray:

When you invite us to worship you in the Spirit of love at the table of the eucharist though we have grown slack in showing hospitality to others, show us your goodness. We pray:

When you invite us, particularly all catechumens, to renounce sin and to be reborn at the font of salvation, show us your way. We pray:

When we are challenged to give witness to your gospel of life on the strength of our faith but fall short, show us your power overcoming our weakness. We pray:

When death brings our earthly pilgrimage to a close, show us your face. (In particular we remember _____ .) We pray:

Presider: God of compassion, you have proven your love for us in Christ. In the richness of your mercy, hear our prayers and deepen our hope in the resurrection. We ask this in Jesus' name.

Third Sunday of Lent (B)

Presider: Christ is the revealed wisdom of God. Let us ask the Spirit to lead us more deeply into this freeing truth.

Petition Leader: Our response is, **"Spirit of all grace, help us."**

Christ cleansed the temple to make it a fit house of prayer. May the Spirit of truth guide the church so that in every way it will be a community of praise and compassion. We pray:

Christ came to cleanse us from sin and all injustice. May the Spirit of Christ purify our hearts and minds that we may live in greater fidelity to the gospel of life. We pray:

Christ freed us from the slavery of death. May those preparing for baptism and reception into the Catholic church be mindful that discipleship is a call to help others find freedom in God's steadfast love. We pray:

Christ crucified is our covenant of love. May we find our spiritual life enriched whenever we proclaim the death of Jesus at the eucharistic table. We pray:

Christ taught that love for God and neighbor are the greatest commandments. May our personal love for God grow into a genuine respect for the rights and needs of others. We pray:

Christ's body was put to death on the cross and was raised on the third day. May our belief in the resurrection of the body sustain us as we mourn the death of those we love (especially _____). We pray:

Presider: God, whose mercy endures forever, listen to our prayers, and by the Word of truth and the Spirit of grace prepare us to be cleansed by the Easter mysteries. We ask this in Jesus' name.

Third Sunday of Lent (C)

Presider: Our faith is meant to bear fruit at every season of life. In faith we ask God to help us fulfill our baptismal vocation.

Petition Leader: Our prayer response today is, **"Gracious God, have mercy!"**

When we overlook God's presence in creation, may the Spirit open our eyes to the ordinary spiritual wonders that surround us. We humbly ask:

When tragedies and natural disasters challenge our faith in God's providential care, may the Spirit of Jesus strengthen the weaknesses in our faith. We humbly ask:

When we feel trapped in unhealthy and oppressive situations, may our faith burst forth in confident appeals to God's liberating love. We humbly ask:

When we feel struck down by human weakness, social injustice, or personal sin, may our faith bring forth the fruit of personal conversion. We humbly ask:

When the cries of the poor and oppressed overwhelm us and challenge our carelessness, may our faith reveal itself in acts of justice for others. We humbly ask:

When the call to discipleship invites us to share in Christ's passion, may our baptismal faith uphold us in peace. We humbly ask:

When death takes from our midst those we love (especially _____), may our faith in God's abounding compassion bring us consolation. We humbly ask:

Presider: God of our ancestors, you have revealed your saving deeds to the children of Israel. Sustain us in mercy and increase our faith through Christ, our Redeemer.

Fourth Sunday of Lent (A)

Option #1: when there are adults preparing for baptism

Presider: Let us pray for spiritual renewal in the church, remembering in a special way those preparing for baptism and confirmation.

Petition Leader: Our prayer response today is: **"Guide us by your Spirit, O Christ."**

For all whose eyes have been opened to recognize Christ as the light of the world and are now preparing for baptism; may the Spirit of God intensify the longing of catechumens to live the gospel of our salvation. We ask in faith:

For their sponsors who have been called to present them at the font of new life; may they be instruments of Christ leading others to the joy of dwelling in God's house. We ask in faith:

For those seeking full communion with the Catholic church; may the Spirit of Christ strengthen their baptismal faith and guide them to the eucharistic table. We ask in faith:

For our youth who are preparing for confirmation; may the Spirit of truth rush upon their hearts and minds and claim their futures for Christ. We ask in faith:

For the pastors of the universal church, Pope *[name]*, and all bishops and priests who have been anointed for service; may their personal love for Christ bring spiritual refreshment to God's people. We ask in faith:

For Christians who have grown slack in faith and morals; may the Spirit renew within them the light of baptismal grace and remove any moral blindness to racism, violence, drug abuse, and gender discrimination. We ask in faith:

For those who have died in Christ; may the Spirit who raised Jesus from the dead fill them with eternal light and life (particularly _____). We ask in faith:

Presider: God of eternal light, you have cast out the power of darkness through the life-giving death of Christ. Continue to draw the church into the fullness of your divine life by the working of your Spirit. Grant our prayers through Christ, our Lord.

Fourth Sunday of Lent (A)

Option #2: when there are no adults preparing for baptism

Presider: Let us pray for spiritual renewal in our church that we may walk by the light of gospel faith.

Petition Leader: Our prayer response today is: **"Guide us by your Spirit, O Christ."**

For the pastors of the universal church, Pope *[name]*, and all bishops and priests who have been anointed for service; may their personal love for Christ bring spiritual refreshment to God's people. We ask in faith:

For all who are preparing for baptism and full communion with the Catholic church; may the Spirit of God lead them in the path of wisdom and truth. We ask in faith:

For our youth who are preparing for confirmation; may the Spirit of truth rush upon their hearts and minds and claim their futures for Christ. We ask in faith:

For Christians who have grown slack in faith and morals; may the Spirit renew within them the light of baptismal grace and remove any moral blindness to racism, violence, drug abuse, and gender discrimination. We ask in faith:

For theologians, catechists, and proclaimers of the gospel; may the Spirit of knowledge and understanding bless their efforts to help the church in teaching about goodness, justice, and truth. We ask in faith:

For those who have died in Christ; may the Spirit who raised Jesus from the dead fill them with eternal light and life (particularly _____). We ask in faith:

Presider: God of eternal light, you have cast out the power of darkness through the life-giving death of Christ. Continue to draw the church into the fullness of your divine life by the working of your Spirit. Grant our prayers through Christ, our Lord.

Fourth Sunday of Lent (B)

Presider: Rejoicing in God's great kindness toward us, let us pray that our lives will be rich in faith, hope, love, and mercy.

Petition Leader: Our response today is, **"God, rich in mercy, hear us."**

May all come to faith and the life of good deeds that renew the world in peace, justice, love, and mercy. Trusting in God's favor, we ask:

May Christians cherish their faith as a gift of God's grace and nourish it by word and sacrament. Trusting in God's favor, we ask:

May the church draw courage from its hope that God's mercy renews all creation in Christ. Trusting in God's favor, we ask:

May the love that is poured into our hearts by the Spirit reveal itself in our willingness to live compassionately. Trusting in God's favor, we ask:

May those who are approaching the life-giving waters of baptism rejoice as they prepare for the sacraments of rebirth. Trusting in God's favor, we ask:

May any who despair of God's mercy because of their sins find spiritual healing in Christ, the sign of God's love. Trusting in God's favor, we ask:

May the dead who have hoped in God's love find eternal life in Christ, who was lifted up for our salvation (especially _____). Trusting in God's favor, we ask:

Presider: God, in every age your mercy has restored the life of your people. Continue to pour new life into us through the gifts of faith, hope, and love so that united with Christ we may praise your goodness forever. Grant this in Jesus' name.

Fourth Sunday of Lent (C)

Presider: In Christ, God continues to welcome sinners with unlimited mercy. With a confident faith let us call upon the Divine Goodness to refresh us.

Petition Leader: Our prayer response is, **"Renew your Spirit in us, O God."**

We call upon God's reconciling love to deliver us from sin and strengthen those preparing for baptism. We pray to our God:

We entrust to the Spirit's care the leadership of the church as it appeals to heads of nations on behalf of peace and nonviolent solutions to conflicts. We pray to our God:

We invoke the Spirit of consolation to bring refreshment in body, mind, and spirit to all who are in periods of recovery from illness. We pray to our God:

We ask for the grace of conversion for all who have been lured away from God's love by drugs, alcohol, or crimes of violence. We pray to our God:

We call down the Spirit of unity and peace to strengthen this community of faith as it prepares to celebrate the Passover of Jesus. We pray to our God:

We pray that the souls of the dead will glory in the Lord of Life (particularly _____). We pray to our God:

Presider: Loving God, nourish our faith with the Word of Life, sustain us by your mercy, and renew us by your Spirit. We ask this in Jesus' name.

Fifth Sunday of Lent (A)

Option #1: when there are adults preparing for baptism

Presider: As we draw closer to Holy Week and Easter, let us intensify our prayers for our spiritual renewal and for those who will receive new life in the Easter sacraments.

Petition Leader: Our prayer response is: **"Spirit of Jesus, be with us!"**

May God guide those who are preparing for baptism. Lead them by the light of faith to Christ, our resurrection and life. We pray:

May God uphold their Christian sponsors and catechists. Preserve in them the grace and peace of Christ. We pray:

May God bestow upon the pastors and ministers of the church a rich faith in Jesus the Messiah. By the Spirit of truth enable them to proclaim courageously the gospel of life. We pray:

May God renew all of the baptized in the peace of Christ. By the sanctifying Spirit may our faith communities be rich havens of compassion and love. We pray:

May God bring consolation to those who mourn. Through the Spirit, the Comforter, help them to find solace in Christ's teachings. We pray:

May God renew our nation morally and spiritually. Under the Holy Spirit's guidance may our national leaders and citizens vigorously pursue justice for the poor and defend human life at all times. We pray:

May God give the dead full redemption in Christ. By the Spirit's power may they be set free and come to life (particularly _____). We pray:

Presider: Loving God, be present in our lives, always drawing us from death to life in Christ through the Holy Spirit. Hear our prayers through Jesus, the Word of Life, who lives and reigns with you and the Holy Spirit, one God, forever and ever.

Fifth Sunday of Lent (A)

Option #2: when there are no adults preparing for baptism

Presider: As we draw closer to Holy Week and Easter, let us intensify our prayers for our spiritual renewal and remember those who are preparing for baptism in other places.

Petition Leader: Our prayer response is: **"Spirit of Jesus, be with us!"**

May God bestow upon the pastors and ministers of the church a rich faith in Jesus the Messiah. By the Spirit of truth enable them to proclaim courageously the gospel of life. We pray:

May God renew all of the baptized in the peace of Christ. By the sanctifying Spirit may our faith communities be rich havens of compassion and love. We pray:

May God uphold those who are preparing for baptism and bless their sponsors and catechists. By the light of faith direct their steps to Christ, our resurrection and life. We pray:

May God bring consolation to those who mourn. Through the Spirit, the Comforter, help them to find solace in Christ's teachings. We pray:

May God renew our nation morally and spiritually. Under the Holy Spirit's guidance may our national leaders and citizens vigorously pursue justice for the poor and defend human life at all times. We pray:

May God give the dead plenteous redemption in Christ. By the Spirit's power may they be set free and come to life (particularly _____). We pray:

Presider: Loving God, be present in our lives, drawing us from death to life in Christ through the Holy Spirit. Grant our prayers through Jesus, the Word of Life, who lives and reigns with you and the Holy Spirit, one God, forever and ever.

Fifth Sunday of Lent (B)

Presider: Knowing that God saves us from death through Christ, let our prayers call upon the Divine Compassion to sustain us.

Petition Leader: Our prayer response today is, **"Compassionate God, help us."**

Uphold in your church a fidelity to your law of love that we may show ourselves to be your faithful people. Believing in your saving love, we pray:

Strengthen all who, out of love for you and your creation, give their lives in service to the gospel. Believing in your saving love, we pray:

Enable our sufferings to witness our discipleship with a crucified Redeemer. Believing in your saving love, we pray:

Sustain those who daily take up the cross of poverty, illness, and rejection. Believing in your saving love, we pray:

Fill with wisdom those who are preparing to profess their faith in Christ at the font of baptism. Believing in your saving love, we pray:

By the grace of the Spirit enliven in every heart a desire to live the covenant of Christ's peace and reconciliation. Believing in your saving love, we pray:

Honor with eternal life the dead who have longed to be drawn into the glory of Christ (especially _____). Believing in your saving love, we pray:

Presider: Saving God, through the dying and rising of Jesus you have destroyed our death and restored our life. With your help may our faith bear fruit and draw all creation into the glory of risen life. We ask this in the name of the One you have glorified, Jesus Christ.

Fifth Sunday of Lent (C)

Presider: The call to share the life of the risen Christ invites us to fix our full attention on the reign of God. As we draw closer to Holy Week and Easter let us intensify our prayer to share in Christ's paschal mystery.

Petition Leader: Our response is, **"Christ, our Savior, hear our prayer."**

That the saving power of Jesus Christ will inspire all believers to foster communities of compassion that renew the hopes of the poor, we pray to the Lord:

That the power of Christ's presence in the eucharistic meal will fortify our longing for God's reign of perfect peace, we pray to the Lord:

That the power flowing from Christ's resurrection will sustain those who suffer from the pain of illness, we pray to the Lord:

That the power of Christ's love for the sinner will be a source of joy for catechumens approaching the waters of baptism and their sponsors, we pray to the Lord:

That the power of the merciful Christ will enable us to be more forgiving and less ready to condemn others to death, particularly by means of the death penalty, we pray to the Lord:

That the power of Christ's risen life will overflow to those who have died (especially _____), we pray to the Lord:

Presider: Jesus, our Redeemer, your word of mercy saved a person condemned to death. By your word save us from death and fill us with the life you won for us on the cross, for you live and reign forever and ever.

Holy Week and Triduum

Passion (Palm) Sunday (A)

Presider: Let us pray for those who walk with Christ crucified.

Petition Leader: Our prayer response will be a moment of silence after each petition. [Leader, allow for a sufficient pause after each petition.]

For the gift of prayer in time of trial and sorrow.

For those whose suffering distances them from needed companions.

For the strength of faith to face resolutely the unknown future.

For those who are betrayed by close friends.

For those who would resort to violence to counter evil.

For those who condemn the innocent and release the guilty.

For those who are tormented in their pain.

For those who feel abandoned or alone at the hour of death.

For those who look to Jesus, at the right hand of the Power, to save them.

Presider: Abba God, Christ bid us to follow. May those who live the passion of Christ experience your saving grace. We ask this in Jesus' name.

Passion (Palm) Sunday (B)

Presider: Let us draw strength from Jesus crucified as we face our own sufferings and death.

Petition Leader: Our prayer response today will be a moment of silent prayer after each petition. [Leader, please allow for a sufficient pause after each petition.]

For the grace to accept resolutely God's will when the cup of suffering cannot pass us by.

For radical trust in God's care when abandoned by friends and family in time of trial.

For Christians who flee from the demands of discipleship with the crucified Christ who is among us in the poor, sick, and needy.

For all who are emotionally and spiritually traumatized by pain.

For the innocent who are without defense and remain falsely convicted of crimes they did not commit.

For those whose bodies will be signed with the cross of Christ in the baptismal waters of Easter.

Presider: Redeeming God, like the Roman centurion, we profess that the crucified Christ is truly your beloved Son. Hear our prayers, offered in the silence of faith, and grant that we may come to the feast of everlasting life. We pray in the name of your obedient servant, Jesus Christ.

Passion (Palm) Sunday (C)

Presider: Let us entrust those who suffer to Christ crucified.

Petition Leader: Our response is a moment of silence after each petition. [Leader, please allow for a sufficient pause after each petition.]

For all who know suffering in body, mind, and spirit.

For innocent persons unjustly deprived of liberty.

For victims of hatred and scorn borne from discrimination.

For those who must face their hour of trial in the strength of faith.

For those subject to public ridicule.

For those whose dignity is violated through physical brutality.

For those who go to their death relying solely on God's mercy.

Presider: God, hear our prayers for all who share in the passion of Jesus. May they also share your consolation. We ask this through Christ, our Redeemer.

Holy Thursday (A, B, and C)

Option #1

Presider: Let us pray.

Petition Leader: The example of Jesus prompts us to pray: **"May our love abound!"**

Christ Jesus, we glory in your cross, which brings new life to the world. Enable us to stand with those whose lives are marked by heavy crosses. We pray:

Servant of God, we celebrate the life and love you share with us in the eucharistic meal. May we share your generosity with the poor and hungry among us. We pray:

Teacher and Savior, you call your disciples to be servants of your Word. May our fidelity to your gospel of life help cleanse our world of violence. We pray:

You became the Covenant of Mercy for sinners. May our works of mercy continue to free the world from sin and death. We pray:

You are the High Priest of the good things to come. Enrich your priestly people with every spiritual blessing in the heavens. We pray:

You rose from the table and entered a garden of anguish. May any who have eaten at your table find consolation in time of trial. We pray:

Presider: Eternal God and Abba of Jesus, you filled your chosen servant with your love—a love that was not overcome by personal suffering and death. Hear our prayers that the love of Christ may abound in us. We ask this in the name of Jesus, our Savior.

Holy Thursday (A, B, and C)

Option #2

Presider: Let us pray.

Petition Leader: We have gathered to proclaim the death of the Lord, and so we call out: **"Servant of God, hear our prayer."**

We remember that you are the new covenant of life for sinners. May your church fearlessly herald your reconciling death. Consoled by your love, we ask:

We remember that your betrayer broke bread with you. May we who eat and drink in your memory not betray you in the person of the poor. Consoled by your love, we ask:

We remember that you came to give your life as a ransom for many. May we be one with you in breaking every form of captivity that oppresses human life. Consoled by your love, we ask:

We remember that you fed the multitudes who were hungry for God's word. May those you have called to be ministers of word and sacrament be signs of your continuing care for us. Consoled by your love, we ask:

We remember that you rose from the table and embraced the hour that was upon you. May those who are at the hour of their death find consolation in your resurrection. Consoled by your love, we ask:

We remember that you are the new Exodus. May your love lead the dead into the New Jerusalem. Consoled by your love, we ask:

Presider: God of tender mercies, Christ taught us to keep his memory. May his words remain part of us that we may have a share in the gospel's blessing. We pray in Jesus' name.

Good Friday (A, B, and C)

[These intercessions have been drawn in part from elements found in prayers for "Various Needs and Occasions" in the Roman Sacramentary. Certain subjects have been selected because of their appropriateness to current lived realities. *Two readers besides the presider are needed.*]

A. For the Church

Presider: Let us pray for the church, the people of God and the body of Christ.

Reader 1: For all who are made sons and daughters of God by baptism;

Reader 2: For Pope *[name]*, servant of the servants of God and universal pastor;

Presider: For Bishop *[name]*, shepherd of the Archdiocese/Diocese of _____;

Reader 1: For all who guide the church as bishops;

Reader 2: For those chosen to minister God's word and sacraments;

Presider: For those called to serve as women and men religious;

Reader 1: For catechists and lay ministers;

Reader 2: And for readers and ministers of the eucharist.

[Period of silent prayer followed by a sung or spoken acclamation by the assembly.]

Presider: God, by the promise you made in the life, death, and resurrection of Jesus, you bring together in your Spirit from all the races, nations, and cultures of the earth a people to be your own. Keep the church faithful to its mission to be leaven in the world, renewing all things in Christ. Enrich all with the very best spiritual gifts, that the church may be a community of compassion and persevering prayer. May all who serve your people perform their ministry with tenderness and kindness. We ask this through Jesus the Christ.

B. For the Unity of Christians

Presider: Let us implore God to bring all Christians together in unity,

Reader 1: that Christian churches may heal from the wounds of division that exist among the followers of Jesus Christ,

Reader 2: and that religious leaders will not extinguish the spirit of ecumenical dialogue kindled by the Second Vatican Council.

[Period of silent prayer followed by a sung or spoken acclamation by the assembly.]

Presider: Compassionate God, bring the hearts of all Christians together in your praise and in common sorrow for our sins. By your love heal all of the divisions that exist among Christians. In the power of your Spirit enlighten Christian leaders to pursue greater unity that all may be fed at one table and all people welcomed to serve in ministries that build up the body of Christ. We ask this in the name of Jesus, who prayed that all may be one.

C. For Those Preparing for Baptism and Full Reception in the Catholic Church

Presider: Let us entrust to the care of the Holy Spirit those who are approaching the life-giving waters of baptism,

Reader 1: and those who are seeking full communion with the Catholic church,

Reader 2: that through the mercy of God they may be responsive to the Spirit of Christ moving them to draw new life from the Easter sacraments.

[Period of silent prayer followed by a sung or spoken acclamation by the assembly.]

Presider: God, Creator of all, you continually bless your church with new members. Deepen the faith of those approaching the waters of baptism that they may have a new birth in the power of your Holy Spirit. Bestow on those to be received into full communion with the Catholic church a full flowering of the faith they received at baptism. We ask this in the name of your life-giving Word, Jesus Christ.

D. For Families

Presider: Let us ask God to strengthen families.

Reader 1: For a deepening of love between husband and wife,

Reader 2: between parents and children, brothers and sisters;

Presider: For a renewal of love in hurting marriages and family relationships, among estranged spouses and alienated relatives;

Reader 1: For the strength to heal from divorce, unemployment, addictions, sickness, and death;

Reader 2: And for the willingness to care for and embrace single parents, unmarried persons, the elderly and widowed, the orphaned, and those who live alone.

[Period of silent prayer followed by a sung or spoken acclamation by the assembly.]

Presider: Loving God, watch over families and guide them with your Spirit. Enable all families to be communities of mutual love. May the dignity of each person be safeguarded and each person's giftedness celebrated. Bless those households that are struggling to cope with separation, sickness, and unemployment. Give every spiritual consolation to those who mourn a loved one. We ask this through Jesus, who came and shared our life even unto death, death on a cross.

E. For Heads of State and Those Who Serve in Public Office

Presider: Let us call upon God to bless those who are leaders of countries.

Reader 1: For all who serve in public office

Reader 2: and for those who carry the responsibility of governing society and protecting human rights and well-being;

Presider: For the President of the United States, the Congress and Supreme Court, governors, and state and local legislators;

Reader 1: For the United Nations and all world leaders;

Reader 2: And for those struggling to lead their people through periods of social reform or out of oppressive regimes and colonialism.

[Period of silent prayer followed by a sung or spoken acclamation by the assembly.]

Presider: God, you call all earthly powers to serve you. Give to those who have the responsibility of leading nations a genuine desire to serve the common good that people everywhere may enjoy freedom and self-determination. Give your wisdom to public leaders so that justice, equality, and a respect for human life may be manifest in all societies. We ask this through Jesus, who came not to be served, but to serve and to give his life as ransom for many.

F. For Peace and Justice

Presider: Let us plead before the God of love to bestow a desire for true peace and justice in every human heart.

Reader 1: For an end to all war, violence, racism, sexism, and discrimination,

Reader 2: that nations will turn their weapons into plowshares, that greed and lust for power will turn into generous service of human needs, and that abuse and exploitation of others will cease.

[Period of silent prayer followed by a sung or spoken acclamation by the assembly.]

Presider: God, lover of peace, you fashioned life, not death. Banish all war and violence from the face of the earth. Transform the hearts of groups that build structures of hate. Empower us to use our voices to advocate an end to policies and spending that ignore the cries of the poor and perpetuate the cycles of death. We ask this in the name of Jesus, the suffering servant, who died as a victim of violence and hatred.

G. For the Hungry, the Homeless, Refugees, and Exiles

Presider: Let us ask God to give us a genuine concern for those who suffer from lack of food;

Reader 1: to rain down blessings upon those who are homeless, refugees, or exiled from their families;

Reader 2: and to give protection to young people who are lost, children who have been abducted, and those who have run away from home.

[Period of silent prayer followed by a sung or spoken acclamation by the assembly.]

Presider: God of all creation, no one is a stranger to you, and no one is ever far from your loving care. In your love watch over the homeless, refugees, and exiles and those separated from their loved ones. Mercifully remove all hunger and starvation from our midst. Inspire all people to work effectively to assure that each individual may have access to the goods of creation. Help us always to show your kindness to strangers and those in need. We ask this in the name of Jesus, who came to save the lost.

H. For the Sick and Dying

Presider: Let us pray that God's compassionate care will be with the sick and dying.

Reader 1: For those who are experiencing a martyrdom in body and spirit;

Reader 2: And for all who feel abandoned in their time of trial, especially for any whose illness is feared by society, and for persons at the point of despair.

[Period of silent prayer followed by a sung or spoken acclamation by the assembly.]

Presider: God of mercy, you call the sick and suffering to share in the passion of Jesus and to serve you in the midst of human weakness. Pour out the grace of the Holy Spirit upon all who suffer in body, mind, and spirit. Sustain the faith and hope of the dying that, sealed with the blood of Christ, they may come before you freed from sin. We ask this in the name of Jesus, who shared our human nature and who learned obedience from what he suffered.

I. For the World's Religions and Those Searching for God

Presider: Let us ask God to bring to perfect fulfillment the faith of the world's religions.

Reader 1: For the Jewish people, who hold fast to the Covenant made with Abraham and to the Law given through Moses,

Reader 2: who have given us the psalms to praise God from the rising to the setting of the sun and the words of the prophets to guide us,

Reader 1: and who have passed on to us the stories of God working through men and women from the beginning of time.

Presider: For all who address God by many names:

Reader 1: As Allah, as the Great Spirit, as Source of all Being, as the Higher Power.

Presider: For those who do not know God's name or experience the movement of faith in their hearts;

Reader 1: For all who are searching for lasting truth and spiritual values;

Reader 2: And for those working to preserve religious freedoms and the primacy of conscience.

[Period of silent prayer followed by a sung or spoken acclamation by the assembly.]

Presider: God, you first revealed your redeeming love to the Israelites. Through Abraham and Sarah you began to fashion a people as your own. May the Jewish people continue to seek you in sincerity of heart and come to acknowledge the full revelation of your redeeming love. Place within every human heart a genuine desire to seek and find you so that all of the living might possess a spiritual voice to praise your glory. We ask this in the name of Jesus, who showed us that your love brings all into being and sustains all life.

Easter Vigil or Easter Sunday (A, B, and C)

Option #1

Presider: Having renewed our faith in God's saving love for us, let us remember the needs of the church and world.

Petition Leader: Our response is: **"Risen Savior, fill us with peace."**

As the church proclaims your glorious resurrection, we pray:

As the community of believers acclaims the gospel of life, we pray:

As we gather at your table with the newly baptized and those received into full communion in the Catholic church, we pray:

As we renew our faith in your steadfast love, we pray:

As we carry the light of your compassion to the sick and elderly, we pray:

As the apostolic church calls the world to new life in your name, especially where there is violence and devastating poverty, we pray:

As we draw hope from your resurrection for our beloved dead (especially _____), we pray:

Presider: God of love and mercy, hear the prayers of your church on this feast of the resurrection, and keep alive in us the peace of the risen Christ, who lives and reigns with you and the Holy Spirit, one God forever and ever.

Easter Vigil or Easter Sunday (A, B, and C)

Option #2

Presider: Let us pray that all the world might share in the glorious freedom of the sons and daughters of God which the risen Christ has won for us.

Petition Leader: Our prayer response is: **"Risen Savior, grant our prayer."**

For the creation that God birthed with love and redeemed with compassion; may all things in heaven and on earth render God fitting praise. As we rejoice in Christ's triumph, we ask:

For those who have been reborn in Christ through these life-giving waters of faith; may the newly baptized hold fast to the life of grace. As we rejoice in Christ's triumph, we ask:

For the church universal, which has renewed its baptismal covenant; may all believers cling to the peace of Christ. As we rejoice in Christ's triumph, we ask:

For Christian households that gather on this feast to share a family meal; may the homes of believers be blessed with joy and love. As we rejoice in Christ's triumph, we ask:

For all who rejoice in the feast of the Lamb; may our celebration of eucharist free us to be servants of the gospel of life. As we rejoice in Christ's triumph, we ask:

For those who have died in the peace of the Savior; may the faithful departed rise at God's word to the glory of the resurrection (especially _____). As we rejoice in Christ's triumph, we ask:

Presider: Loving God, may we never cease to praise you for the gift of redemption. Receive the prayers of your church in the name of the Christ, the first-born of the dead.

Easter Vigil or Easter Sunday (A, B, and C)

Option #3

Presider: With Easter joy we pray.

Petition Leader: Our response is, **"May all praise your glory, O Christ."**

For the church as it heralds the gospel of life throughout the world; may the Spirit of Christ prepare every heart to receive the good news. We pray:

For the newly baptized; may their sharing in the banquet of the Lamb be a rich source of grace and peace. We pray:

For those received into full communion in the Catholic church; may the eucharist strengthen our unity. We pray:

For all the baptized; may our participation in Jesus' paschal mystery inspire us to live more reverently. We pray:

For those who are still far from the peace of the risen Christ; may the Spirit stir in the hearts of enemies a desire for harmony and friendship. We pray:

For those who have died in the joyful hope of eternal life; may they be found rejoicing in the reign of heaven (especially _____). We pray:

Presider: Loving God, may our gathering at this table of unity fill us with longing for the feast of heaven. We ask that you receive our prayers in the name of the risen Savior, Jesus Christ.

Easter Season

Second Sunday of Easter (A)

Presider: Let us pray in the Spirit of the One who is risen.

Petition Leader: Our response is, **"God of love, hear us."**

For the community of believers in Jesus' resurrection, that it will remain strong in love and faithful to the gospel of salvation. We pray:

For newly baptized adults, that they will continue to draw on the life of the risen Christ who abides among us in word and sacrament. We pray:

For those who doubt the good news of salvation, that the Spirit will guide them into the truth of faith. We pray:

For those who continue to suffer for the faith, especially in areas hostile to Christianity, that they will be guarded with God's saving power. We pray:

For persons confined by fear, that God's freeing love will lead them to the peace of the risen Christ. We pray:

For those who have believed in Christ's resurrection and have died, that they will be counted among the blessed in the reign of glory (particularly _____). We pray:

Presider: God, in your abounding mercy, sustain in your church the gifts of faith, hope, and love which give us new life in Christ, who lives and reigns forever and ever.

Second Sunday of Easter (B)

Presider: Rejoicing in the Spirit of truth who raised Jesus from the dead, let us pray to bear witness to the resurrection.

Petition Leader: Our prayer response is, **"God of mercy, receive our prayer."**

Enable us to be generous distributors of your abundant gifts, especially to the needy among us. As we rejoice in the Spirit of Christ, we pray:

By your word of life, break through our fears and empower us to be instruments of justice. As we rejoice in the Spirit of Christ, we pray:

Through this sacred meal, nourish our faith in the Christ who has conquered the powers of sin and death. As we rejoice in the Spirit of Christ, we pray:

Begotten through the waters of baptism, may your sons and daughters be gathered into a single household of faith and love. As we rejoice in the Spirit of Christ, we pray:

Sustained by the promise of a more glorious world free of all affliction, may those whose lives are passing away be consoled by the Easter proclamation. As we rejoice in the Spirit of Christ, we pray:

Trusting in the truth of your gospel, may the dead who hoped in your mercy find contentment in the reign of heaven (especially _____). As we rejoice in the Spirit of Christ, we pray:

Presider: Gracious God, Giver of Life, in Christ your church raises its voice in prayer. Hear us as we call on your mercy and uphold us in the Spirit of the risen Savior. Grant our prayer in Jesus' name.

Second Sunday of Easter (C)

Presider: Let us pray in the Spirit of the One who lives.

Petition Leader: Our prayer response is: **"Risen Savior, hear us!"**

That the church reborn in baptismal waters will carry on the healing mission of Christ in the midst of a troubled world. We pray:

That the Spirit and our Christian witness will continue to draw more people to Christ and the gospel of peace. We pray:

That our joyful praise of Christ's victory at the table of the eucharist will be a source of grace for the newly baptized. We pray:

That those who entertain doubts of Christ's victory over death will be guided by the Spirit to true faith. We pray:

That the One who is the First and Last will dispel any fear from the hearts of those for whom this life is passing away. We pray:

That the dead who carried the hope of resurrection in their hearts will rise at the word of Christ to the glory of the resurrection (especially _____). We pray:

Presider: God, whose mercy is everlasting, you have given Christ the power over sin and death. Accept your church's praise and receive our prayers in the Savior's name, who lives and reigns with you and the Holy Spirit, one God forever and ever.

Third Sunday of Easter (A)

Presider: Let us pray that the world will live in greater reverence for God and God's creation.

Petition Leader: Our response is, **"Saving God, give us wisdom."**

We implore God to uphold Pope *[name]* and the church's bishops as they proclaim the wonders of God's mercy. We pray:

We intercede on behalf of all who are instruments of violence; may the power of God's love, confirmed in the resurrection of Christ, lead to conversion of heart and mind. We pray:

We ask that our eyes and hearts remain open to the mystery of God's redeeming love breaking into our lives. We pray:

We petition God to lavish the Spirit of the risen Christ upon all judicial systems that they may speak in the name of life and affirm the dignity of every citizen. We pray:

We ask God to bless the church's ministry to the unchurched, that all may come to believe the good news. We pray:

We entrust to God those who have died with faith and hope centered in the victory of Christ (especially _____); may they rejoice in the reign of heaven. We pray:

Presider: Redeeming God, receive the prayers of your church, and by your Spirit empower us to live the mystery of Christ. Grant this through Christ, in whose name we break your life-giving bread.

Third Sunday of Easter (B)

Presider: Believing that Christ is in our midst through the Holy Spirit, let us raise our voices to intercede with the just Savior.

Petition Leader: Our prayer response today is, **"Receive our prayers, Lord."**

May the church continue to witness to its belief in the resurrection by its commitment to uphold the gift of life for all persons. As we rejoice in your triumph, we pray:

May the one sacrifice of Christ that has redeemed all humanity inspire believers to pursue integrity of word and deed in their lives. As we rejoice in your triumph, we pray:

May all who taste the goodness and peace of Christ in this gathering be built up as a community of compassion for the needy. As we rejoice in your triumph, we pray:

May the Spirit of truth guide to true faith those who struggle with doubt in the resurrection. As we rejoice in your triumph, we pray:

May Christian legislators witness to the resurrection of Jesus by supporting quality health care for all people, especially infants and children. As we rejoice in your triumph, we pray:

May the dying and rising of Christ transform the sadness of death into sheer joy for all who have died (especially _____). As we rejoice in your triumph, we pray:

Presider: God, ever rich in love for your people, receive the prayers of your church which we make through our intercessor, Jesus Christ, the first-born of many sisters and brothers.

Third Sunday of Easter (C)

Presider: With the resurrection of Christ, our hope of resurrection has dawned. Let us intercede with the Lamb of God, who is the cause of our rejoicing.

Petition Leader: Our prayer response is: **"Christ victor, hear our prayer!"**

The resurrection of Jesus has brought joy to the homes of all believers. May our homes be rich in the peace of the risen Christ. We pray:

The disciples received power in the name of the risen Christ. In Christ's name may the church courageously herald the gospel of life despite opposition to it. We pray:

The Holy Spirit joins our spirit in witnessing to Christ. May we use the Spirit's gifts of faith, hope, and love to build up the faith of the newly baptized. We pray:

The risen Christ blessed the efforts of the early church in bringing others to faith. May the church's ministry of evangelization bring more lives to Christ and the eucharistic meal. We pray:

Christ instructed Simon Peter to feed the flock. May Pope *[name]* and the bishops of the church nourish the faithful through their witness to Christ's compassion for the suffering poor. We pray:

All the voices of heaven were seen worshipping the living God and the Lamb. May our beloved dead be counted among them (especially _____). We pray:

Presider: Loving God, in Christ's victory you have turned our mourning into dancing. Sustain in your church the Spirit of love that we may praise you unceasingly in the company of Christ. We ask this in Jesus' name.

Fourth Sunday of Easter (A)

Presider: Let us pray for the good of all.

Petition Leader: Our prayer response is, **"Jesus, our Way, guide us."**

We turn our hearts toward the new creation that Christ has achieved in his dying and rising. May we pursue the fullness of life in the Spirit of love. We pray:

We rejoice that the Keeper of the Gate has swept aside the barrier of death for Jesus crucified. May the community of believers confront the barriers to peace through the power of the cross. We pray:

We ask for the grace of conversion for all who perpetuate the cycle of violence through revenge and retaliation. May God's Spirit enable all to be forgiving of others. We pray:

We have accepted the Word of mercy and break bread in memory of Christ. May our lifestyles draw others to the mystery of God in Christ. We pray:

We entrust to God the newly baptized. May they dwell in the house of God all the days of their lives. We pray:

We return to God all our beloved dead (especially _____). May they find refreshment in the reign of heaven. We pray:

Presider: God, you have restored our life in Christ. Receive our prayers that the Savior's healing mission may continue in your church. We ask this in Jesus' name.

Fourth Sunday of Easter (B)

Presider: Because we are God's children by water and the Spirit we confidently pray for the life of the world in the name of Jesus.

Petition Leader: Our response today is, **"In Christ's name, hear us."**

We profess Christ to be the cornerstone of our faith. May Christ's legacy of love be our inspiration for renewing gospel values within our culture. As we rejoice in God's saving love, we pray:

We acknowledge the power of the risen Christ as the source of healing for the world. May the Spirit of Jesus bless the work of all who labor to discover cures for deadly diseases. As we rejoice in God's saving love, we pray:

We look to Christ to gather all peoples into a family of unity and peace. May our efforts to promote unity within the church and world be guided by the Holy Spirit. As we rejoice in God's saving love, we pray:

We trust in God's care to sustain the church when it experiences hostility for proclaiming the gospel of life. May we find courage to do good for those most in need. As we rejoice in God's saving love, we pray:

We believe that in Christ we find wholeness in body, mind, and spirit. May we cooperate with the grace of God and foster morally and spiritually healthy lifestyles. As we rejoice in God's saving love, we pray:

We are consoled by our hope to be like Christ in the glory of the resurrection. May the dead find mercy in the One who laid down his life for all peoples (especially _____). As we rejoice in God's saving love, we pray:

Presider: God of all creation, you have given Christ the power over life and death. In the name of your Beloved, hear our prayers and sustain in us the joy of Easter.

Fourth Sunday of Easter (C)

Presider: In Easter hope we pray.

Petition Leader: Our response is: **"Uphold us, saving God."**

That the church will be strong in its proclamation of the gospel of life even when confronted by hostile opposition. With confident faith we ask:

That missionaries will be strengthened by the Holy Spirit as they carry the message of God's compassionate love throughout the world. With confident faith we ask:

That all who hear the word of God today will grow stronger as a community of peace formed for Christ from every nation, race, and language. With confident faith we ask:

That murder victims who suffered from religious persecution, racial hatred, or sexual abuse will be led by the risen Christ to streams of life-giving water in the reign of heaven. With confident faith we ask:

That Christians who continue to perpetuate racism and sexual discrimination in private and public life will find themselves confronted by the power of the risen Christ and be healed. With confident faith we ask:

That the dead will be cleansed by the life-giving death of Christ and find eternal rest (particularly _____). With confident faith we ask:

Presider: God, indeed you show no partiality based on race or culture, for in Christ you gather all people into one. Sustain your church as a community of peace and prayer, and lead us to the fullness of life in Christ. We ask this in Jesus' name.

Fifth Sunday of Easter (A)

Presider: Let us pray that our love will serve the needs of all.

Petition Leader: Our prayer response is, **"Christ, our Life, hear us."**

At baptism we were anointed to be a holy priesthood. May the power of love free us to give ourselves completely to the mystery of Christ. We pray:

At confirmation we were sealed in the Spirit and sent to proclaim the good news. May our use of the Spirit's rich gifts bring others to the font of salvation. We pray:

At table we share the bread of life. May we not neglect the human needs of the elderly, especially those who are financially poor women. We pray:

At the profession of marriage or religious vows, men and women promise to follow the way of love revealed in Christ. May the fidelity of spouses and consecrated religious build up the body of Christ. We pray:

At ordination our clergy are commissioned for service. May the ministry of bishops, priests, and deacons continue to spread the word of God's healing love. We pray:

At death our bodies return to the earth. May our beloved dead rise at Christ's word to the glory of the resurrection (especially _____). We pray:

Presider: God, in Christ we are built up in the Spirit to be a living temple of praise. Hear our prayers and keep us faithful to our calling. We ask this in the name of the risen Savior.

Fifth Sunday of Easter (B)

Presider: United to Christ in the Spirit of love, let us pray that our lives will bear abundant fruit for God's reign of peace, justice, holiness, and compassion.

Petition Leader: Our prayer response today is, **"Gracious God, may we abide in love."**

Lead us by the Spirit of truth to the beauty of your saving Word that we may be cleansed from all evil. As we rejoice in the resurrection of Jesus, we pray:

Guide heads of nations and legislative bodies by your Spirit of wise counsel that they may foster compassion in the hearts of citizens. As we rejoice in the resurrection of Jesus, we pray:

Empower church leaders through your sacred Spirit to promote the dignity of every person, thereby witnessing to a genuine love for our neighbor. As we rejoice in the resurrection of Jesus, we pray:

By the healing power of the Spirit reunite to the vine of Christ any who are alienated from the community of faith by divorce and remarriage. As we rejoice in the resurrection of Jesus, we pray:

Through the Spirit of unity draw diverse races and cultures into common bonds of respect and care. As we rejoice in the resurrection of Jesus, we pray:

Sustain through the consoling Spirit all who grieve the loss of a loved one (especially the families of _____). As we rejoice in the resurrection of Jesus, we pray:

Presider: God, may your church abide in the saving love of Christ and its prayers be found acceptable in your sight. We pray in the name of the risen Redeemer, Jesus Christ.

Fifth Sunday of Easter (C)

Presider: Let us pray that God's gracious love and mercy will accompany us on our pilgrim way.

Petition Leader: Our response is: **"Bless and keep us, Lord."**

For the leadership in our local church and parishes; may Bishop *[name]*, with all clergy and pastoral ministers, continue to build up the Archdiocese/Diocese of _____ to be a people of justice and compassion. We pray:

For couples preparing for marriage; may Christ's love be the root and foundation of the life they look forward to sharing as husband and wife. We pray:

For married persons, especially Christian spouses; may the mutual love of husband and wife provide our society with a strong witness to the gospel. We pray:

For single persons, the widowed, separated, and divorced; may discipleship with the risen Christ continue to be their source of spiritual and emotional strength. We pray:

For those who have died in Christ; may they be with God forever in the New Jerusalem (particularly _____). We pray:

Presider: Loving God, you have glorified Christ through the resurrection. May our love witness to our discipleship and bring you the fullness of praise you deserve. Grant our prayers through Christ, our Resurrection and Life.

Sixth Sunday of Easter (A)

Presider: Let us pray that the sanctifying Spirit will keep us united in Christ, our way to eternal glory.

Petition Leader: Our response is, **"Bless us with your Spirit, O God."**

For the community of believers baptized into Christ; may the Spirit of the Lord inspire our prayers of faith and hope. We pray:

For the spiritual gift of discernment; may the Spirit's good counsel enable us to recognize genuinely worthwhile labor on behalf of God's kingdom. We pray:

For the gifts of knowledge and understanding of God's truth; may the Paraclete direct our feet into the way of peace. We pray:

For missionaries who proclaim Christ to the nations; may the anointing Spirit guide their ministry. We pray:

For gentleness and humility in our lives; may the Spirit of Jesus enable us to build communities of mutual care and respect. We pray:

For all who have died in Christ (particularly _____). May they be given life in the realm of the spirit. We pray:

Presider: God, we believe that Christ is the One who has life. Hear our prayers, and by the Spirit's power pour into our hearts the life of the risen Savior, in whose name we pray.

Sixth Sunday of Easter (B)

Presider: Assured by Christ that whatever we ask in his name will be granted by our God, let us pray above all else to be more loving.

Petition Leader: Our response today is, **"Give us the Spirit of love, Lord."**

May the ministry of Pope *[name]* and the church's bishops reach out to all people who seek God's saving love in Christ. As we proclaim the rising of Jesus, we ask:

May the church's sacramental and pastoral ministers rejoice in the Spirit's gifts of faith and love bestowed upon God's people. As we proclaim the rising of Jesus, we ask:

May all peoples receive with open hearts and minds the gift of redemption in Jesus Christ. As we proclaim the rising of Jesus, we ask:

May we work to replace hostility with the friendship and peace of the risen Christ, especially in our homes. As we proclaim the rising of Jesus, we ask:

May our knowledge of God's love guide our faith communities as we build up the unity and diversity of the universal church. As we proclaim the rising of Jesus, we ask:

May Christ bring God's reconciling peace to those who grieve their offenses against others, especially those imprisoned for crimes of violence. As we proclaim the rising of Jesus, we ask:

Presider: God of joy and mercy, we are grateful for the gift of your redeeming love. May we abide in its wonder and peace as friends and disciples of the risen Savior, in whose name we pray.

Sixth Sunday of Easter (C)

Presider: Christ died and rose that we might have life to the full. Let us pray that we will be faithful to the gospel of peace and share in risen life.

Petition Leader: Our prayer response is: **"Christ, our Peace, hear our prayer."**

For the church as it builds on the foundations of faith set by the apostles; may our profession of faith sustain the unity of the church. We pray:

For Pope *[name]* and the bishops of the church in their teaching mission; may the Spirit of wisdom be with them to guide the community of believers into the new millennium. We pray:

For theologians and catechists in the church; may their teachings and writings enrich the faith and vision of the people of God. We pray:

For all who worry about doing right; may they find the gospel an invitation to worship God free from fear and anxiety. We pray:

For all of us as we strive to put Christ's farewell gift of peace into daily practice; may the eucharist be our model for living in harmony with all creation. We pray:

For the faithful departed who longed to see the city of God (particularly _____); may they be welcomed by the risen Christ into the heavenly Jerusalem. We pray:

Presider: Merciful God, in your justice you have brought new life to sinners through the dying and rising of Jesus. May the new life we have received in baptism come to its fullness in the city of praise. Grant this in Jesus' name.

Ascension of the Lord (A, B, and C)

Option #1

Presider: On this festival day, let us ask Christ to mediate on our behalf with God, our Creator.

Petition Leader: Our prayer response is: **"Risen Savior, hear our prayer."**

May your ascension into glory inspire your church to resound with praise and adoration. Send us your Spirit that we may worship in truth and love. We ask in faith:

May your exaltation to the right hand of God bring us every spiritual benefit. Send us the Spirit of holiness that we may be faithful disciples. We ask in faith:

May your return to your Abba prompt us to seek your glory. Send us the Spirit to lead us into all truth. We ask in faith:

May your authority over the powers of sin and death fill us with hope. Send us the promised Paraclete to sustain us on our pilgrimage. We ask in faith:

May your glorious ascension fill us with a deeper respect for human life. Send us the Spirit of wisdom and courage to help us renew all humanity by your Word. We ask in faith:

May your eternal reign of mercy and love claim the divine life for all the dead. Send us the Spirit of consolation to comfort us in time of trial and sorrow. We ask in faith:

Presider: Abba God, you have given to Christ full authority over your new creation. May our prayers come before you through the One who sits at your right hand, Jesus Christ, our Lord.

Ascension of the Lord (A, B, and C)

Option #2

Presider: Rejoicing in Christ's exaltation into glory, let us ask our Mediator with God to pour forth the promised Spirit.

Petition Leader: Our prayer response on this festival day is, **"Christ, strengthen us with your Spirit."**

Christ Jesus, we celebrate your victory over sin and death. May the power of the Spirit safeguard our lives in your grace and peace. As we rejoice in your ascension, we pray:

Beloved of God, you have ascended into the heavenly temple. Fill us with the riches of your Spirit that we may offer you fitting praise. As we rejoice in your ascension, we pray:

Compassionate Savior, you have left your church a legacy of love. Empower us through the Paraclete to carry on your mission of mercy to all peoples. As we rejoice in your ascension, we pray:

Word of Life, you have been given full authority over the new creation. Re-create us in your own Spirit that we may hasten the reign of enduring peace. As we rejoice in your ascension, we pray:

Our mediator at the right hand of the Power, you have not left us without hope. May the sanctifying Spirit lead all peoples to the fountain of salvation. As we rejoice in your ascension, we pray:

Alpha and Omega, all time belongs to you. By the presence of your Spirit help us to use wisely the temporal gifts you give us. As we rejoice in your ascension, we pray:

Presider: God of glory and Abba of Jesus, you have raised up Christ to be our advocate with you. May the prayer of your Beloved on our behalf bring the Spirit to rest upon us. Receive our prayers through Christ, our Savior.

Seventh Sunday of Easter (A)

Presider: Let us pray to Christ who intercedes for us at God's right hand.

Petition Leader: Our prayer response is, **"May all praise your glory, O Christ."**

Through the gift of the Spirit may your faithful people be united in prayer. We ask in faith:

Through the gift of redemption may all the baptized witness to the holiness of life. We ask in faith:

Through the gift of your Word may the world be re-created in peace. We ask in faith:

Through the gifts of grace may those who search for God be led to Christ. We ask in faith:

Through the gift of love may those approaching marriage, ordination, and profession of religious vows bring greater honor to the Savior's name. We ask in faith:

Through the Spirit's comfort may the sick and suffering find strength. We ask in faith:

Through the resurrection and ascension of Jesus may the dead come to dwell in God's presence forever (especially _____). We ask in faith:

Presider: God, we are yours for time and eternity. May our unlimited confidence in your mercy be sustained by the Spirit's presence. We pray in the name of the One you have glorified, Jesus Christ.

Seventh Sunday of Easter (B)

Presider: Let us pray to be sanctified by the Spirit of truth that we may live in the love of Christ all our days.

Petition Leader: Our prayer response is, **"Loving God, pour forth your Spirit."**

May God's love for the poor and oppressed be perfected in us through the anointing Spirit. As we rejoice in Christ's exaltation in glory, we pray:

May the word of God be the root and foundation of our worshiping communities. As we rejoice in Christ's exaltation in glory, we pray:

May the indwelling Spirit fashion us into a people of nonviolence. As we rejoice in Christ's exaltation in glory, we pray:

May the apostolic ministry of the church leaders, clergy, and religious provide inspiring witness to God's enduring kindness. As we rejoice in Christ's exaltation in glory, we pray:

May the Spirit of truth guide the deliberations of national judicial bodies that they may be servants of life and health for all citizens. As we rejoice in Christ's exaltation in glory, we pray:

May the vitalizing Spirit of Jesus beget in every human heart a desire to know God and to seek goodness. As we rejoice in Christ's exaltation in glory, we pray:

May the Spirit, who raised Jesus from the dead, bring to life all who have died trusting in God's love (especially_____). As we rejoice in Christ's exaltation in glory, we pray:

Presider: Compassionate God, out of love for the sinful you sent Jesus Christ as the prophet of your boundless mercy. May we live by the Spirit of love and find true intimacy with the world's Redeemer. Grant our prayer in Jesus' name.

Seventh Sunday of Easter (C)[+]

Presider: Ascended into glory, Christ has become our advocate before the throne of grace. May the promised Spirit of Christ sustain us in peace until the Morning Star rises on the last day.

Petition Leader: Our prayer response is: **"Christ, send us your Spirit."**

To the church that longs for your return, we pray:

To all who work to restore unity to the churches, we pray:

To Christians who thirst for your life and have accepted baptism, we pray:

To all who proclaim your death and resurrection at eucharist, we pray:

To religious whom you have called to a life of contemplative prayer, we pray:

To non-Christians who are open to hearing the church's proclamation, we pray:

To all who share your martyrdom in body, mind, and spirit, we pray:

To those who are persecuted for calling the world to justice in your name, we pray:

To the faithful who have longed to be in your company and have now died, we pray:

Presider: Loving God, Christ has revealed the limitlessness of your love for us. Through the promised Spirit and persevering prayer draw us more deeply into the mystery of your love. Grant this in the name of David's offspring, Jesus Christ.

+ These petitions are designed to be read as a litany. The proclamation should move quickly but not in a rushed or hurried manner. It is a companion piece to the intercessions for the following Sunday, Pentecost.

Pentecost (A, B, and C)+

Option #1

Presider: Let us invoke the Spirit, the soul's delightful guest, to fill us with the life of the risen Christ.

Petition Leader: Our invocation today is: **"Come, sanctifying Spirit!"**

To all who wait on you in prayer . . .

To those joined as one in the body of Christ through the waters of baptism . . .

To those who feast on the Word of Life in the eucharistic banquet . . .

To those who seek your pardon and peace as they confess their sins . . .

To those whose faith in Christ has been sealed through confirmation . . .

To those bound together in the covenant of marriage and to those preparing for marriage . . .

To those consecrated to Christ and service to the church by ordination and religious vows . . .

To the sick, aged, and infirmed who seek healing, comfort, and forgiveness . . .

To all who are called to teach and proclaim the good news of salvation . . .

To those who sit in death's shadow awaiting the dawn of eternal light (especially _____) . . .

Presider: Gracious God, through Christ you have poured the Spirit of love into our hearts. May the Spirit uphold us and bring our prayer to perfection before you. Grant this through Christ, our Lord.

+ Like the petitions for the Seventh Sunday of Easter (Cycle C), these are styled to be a litany embracing the sacramental life of the church. They should be proclaimed joyfully and swiftly, but not in a rushed or hurried manner.

Pentecost (A, B, and C)+

Option #2

Presider: The Spirit that God gives us is no cowardly Spirit. Let us pray to be strong, loving, and wise in furthering the gospel of Christ.

Petition Leader: Our invocation today is, **"Come, Giver of Life!"**

To the church as it heralds the gospel of salvation . . .

To the leaders of nations as they address the issues of life and death . . .

To the heads of household who seek your wisdom in guiding their children . . .

To those who safeguard citizens through police and fire protection agencies . . .

To all who pray for healing in time of illness . . .

To those who serve your people as religious leaders, teachers, and theologians . . .

To all who work to improve the quality of life for the most needy . . .

To all who dedicate their time in the healing professions . . .

To us as we gather in prayer at this table of life . . .

Presider: God, Giver of every worthwhile gift, we praise you for the world's salvation. May the Spirit enlighten our hearts, inspire our prayers, and unite us to Christ, in whose name we invoke your saving grace.

+ Like the petitions for the Seventh Sunday of Easter (Cycle C), these are styled to be a litany. They should be proclaimed joyfully and swiftly, but not in a rushed or hurried manner.

Pentecost (A, B, and C)+

Option #3

Presider: Let us pray that the fires of the Spirit's love will rest upon us.

Petition Leader: Our invocation today is, **"Fill us, O Spirit of God!"**

Come, Spirit, kindle in us the fire of fidelity to the word of God. We pray:

Come, Spirit, kindle in us the fire of a courageous faith. We pray:

Come, Spirit, kindle in us the fire of justice for the poor. We pray:

Come, Spirit, kindle in us the fire of compassionate service. We pray:

Come, Spirit, kindle in us the fire of unceasing prayer. We pray:

Come, Spirit, kindle in us the fire of reverence for all life. We pray:

Come, Spirit, kindle in us the fire of unity and peace. We pray:

Come, Spirit, kindle in us the fires of a new pentecost. We pray:

Presider: Spirit of God, giver of all life, beget in us the mystery of Christ, and lead us always to the fullness of truth that holds eternal joy. We ask you to come as the Creator's gift in the name of Jesus.

+ Like the petitions for the Seventh Sunday of Easter (Cycle C), these are styled to be a litany. They should be proclaimed joyfully and swiftly, but not in a rushed or hurried manner.

Solemnities and Feasts of the Lord

Trinity Sunday (A)

Presider: Assured of God's love for the world in Christ, let us invoke the Spirit of God that grace and peace may abound among us.

Petition Leader: Our response is: **"Spirit of love, be with us."**

For God's help to break away from hatred that leads to death; may the Spirit help us to take up the way of love that leads to eternal life. We pray:

For Christian churches throughout the world; may our worship of the one God through Christ and in the Holy Spirit lead us to deeper unity. We pray:

For greater harmony and peace among members of the Catholic church; may we come to embrace our rich diversity and our common profession of faith as the work of the Spirit. We pray:

For an increase of the virtues of kindness and fidelity in all marriages; may the mutual love of husband and wife be rooted in Christ's love for us. We pray:

For the grace to renew societies in Christ's love; may the Spirit help us to dismantle racism, destruction of human life, and abuse of creation. We pray:

For the dead who have believed that all come to life in Christ; may the Spirit unite them to the glory of God (especially_____). We pray:

Presider: Gracious God, pour the Spirit of love into our hearts that we may be united to Christ and to each other in the bond of peace. May our prayers be acceptable to you in the name of your only Son, our Redeemer, Jesus Christ.

Trinity Sunday (B)

Presider: Let us pray to be led by the Spirit so that as God's daughters and sons we may carry out all that Christ has commanded.

Petition Leader: Our prayer response today is, **"God, guide us in all our ways."**

May our worship of our Creator lead to greater reverence for the creation birthed with love. We ask in faith:

May the honor we give to Christ, truly God and truly human, draw others to discipleship with the Savior of all humankind. We ask in faith:

May the glory we offer the Holy Spirit enable all God-centered people to live devoutly all the days of their life. We ask in faith:

May our reverence for the Trinity inspire the church to foster unity among all peoples so that peace may prosper everywhere. We ask in faith:

May the greatness of God revealed in the saving mission of Christ and the Spirit be our source of hope in time of trial. We ask in faith:

May all who are baptized in the name of the Trinity be brought together in one communion of love to profess the one life-giving faith. We ask in faith:

May the faithful departed come to rejoice in the Trinity's unending love (especially _____). We ask in faith:

Presider: Loving God, we acknowledge your love revealed to us in the glory of Christ and the splendor of your Spirit. Receive our prayers and grant that we may come to the inheritance held out to us in Christ. We pray as your adopted children in Christ's name.

Trinity Sunday (C)

Presider: Jesus, the Word and Wisdom of God, has assured us that the Spirit of truth will guide us in every way. With a confident faith, let us pray.

Petition Leader: Our prayer response today is: **"Lead us to all truth, O Spirit!"**

For the church as it (moves toward the new millennium/begins the new millennium); may the Spirit empower it to discern God's creative will. We pray:

For all baptized Christians who profess faith in a Trinity of Persons; may the Spirit bring the disciples of Jesus together in common praise of God. We pray:

For those who approach God through other faith traditions and beliefs; may the Spirit direct their steps to the fullness of God's glory. We pray:

For all of us gathered at table to worship the living God; may the grace in which we now stand free us to live gospel virtues. We pray:

For all involved in scientific and medical research; may the Spirit give right judgment to all who can affect the forces of earthly life. We pray:

For those committed to improving the environment; may the begetting Spirit delight in their efforts to preserve the earth's resources. We pray:

Presider: Creator God, ever-living and true, you have revealed your love for us through Word and Spirit. Hear our prayers and guide us in right paths to the glory you share with the Son and the Holy Spirit forever and ever.

Body and Blood of Christ (A)+

Presider: Strengthened by God's word, let us pray.

Petition Leader: Our response to today's petitions is: **"Give us your Living Bread, O God."**

For all who are called to a ministry of teaching in the church; may catechists, homilists, theologians, and bishops nourish the community of believers with the bread of God's word. We pray:

For any whose spiritual journey has brought them to the desert; may the word of God sustain them. We pray:

For all who feast on the Bread of Life; may those who have been recently received at the table of the eucharist be fortified spiritually. We pray:

For those who struggle to believe that Christ is the Living Bread come down from heaven; may the Holy Spirit lead all spiritual seekers to the fullness of truth. We pray:

For all of us who have gathered at this table to share in the one bread and the one cup of blessing; may our communion with Christ enable us to share God's love with one another. We pray:

For those who were nourished on the Living Bread during their earthly journey; may the faithful departed be raised on the last day. We pray:

Presider: God, Giver of all good gifts, you rained down manna in the desert, and in the fullness of time you have given us Jesus Christ, the Living Bread. May our prayers come before you through the mercy of Christ, who intercedes for us at your right hand now and forever.

+ May also be used in Votive Mass of the Eucharist.

Body and Blood of Christ (B)+

Presider: Christ has cleansed us in the waters of baptism and renews with us the covenant of redemption in this sacred meal. Let us pray that our lives will be fortified on these sacraments of love.

Petition Leader: Our prayer response today is, **"Living God, hear our prayer!"**

May the Spirit of Love enrich our Bishop *[name]* and the Archdiocese/Diocese of _____ as our local church joins in Christ's sacrifice of peace. In faith we ask:

May the church's reverence of the Word of salvation fortify human hopes in God's eternal mercies. In faith we ask:

May all who minister God's word and sacraments, particularly within our parish family, perform their work with the gentleness and compassion of Christ. In faith we ask:

May our eucharistic banquet purify Christian communities of all racism and discrimination among the members of the body of Christ. In faith we ask:

May our sharing in the cup of blessing free us to continue our labors on behalf of all who thirst for justice. In faith we ask:

May the healing love of Christ offered in these sacred signs bring consolation to the sick and dying. In faith we ask:

May all the dead who feasted on the body and blood of Christ come to their eternal inheritance in the reign of God (especially_____). In faith we ask:

Presider: Sustaining God, in Christ you have called us to be your priestly people. As we intercede on each other's behalf may your Spirit sanctify us through Christ, our Passover and our Peace.

+ May also be used in Votive Mass of the Eucharist or Precious Blood.

Body and Blood of Christ (C)+

Presider: Let us pray.

Petition Leader: Remembering that Christ abides among us, let us call out: **"Living Bread, Living Word, hear us!"**

Mindful that it is not on bread alone that we live, but on God's word, may we nourish our world with the good news of salvation. We pray:

Renewed in body, mind, and spirit through the covenant in Christ's blood, may we be fortified to build covenant communities that renew the hopes of the poor. We pray:

Gathered at table to be strengthened by this Living Bread, may we be alive in the Spirit of mercy and peace and dead to sin. We pray:

Called to be one with the Mediator of the New Covenant, may we use our voices to mediate the needs of those thirsting for justice. We pray:

Summoned to worship the living God, may we be blessed with every spiritual gift and come to the eternal inheritance held out to us in Christ. We pray:

Invited to share the Bread of Affliction and the Cup of Sorrows, may our sharing in Jesus' paschal mystery seat us at the banquet table where Lazarus is no longer poor. We pray:

Filled with good things through God's tender compassion, may those who have eaten the Bread of Life be filled with eternal life (particularly _____). We pray:

Presider: Nurturing God, you alone can satisfy our hungry hearts. May we be sustained by the Christ, our Living Bread, in whose name we make intercession, for he lives and reigns with you and the Holy Spirit, one God forever and ever.

+ May also be used in Votive Mass of the Eucharist or Precious Blood.

Sacred Heart of Jesus (A, B, and C)[+]

Presider: Because we are a people sacred to God, let us pray for gifts in keeping with the mind and heart of Christ.

Petition Leader: Our response is: **"God of love, hear us."**

For the gift of a courageous faith that witnesses to the good news of salvation, we pray:

For the gift of hope that God's tender mercy accompanies us through life, we pray:

For the gift of an unwavering love that our lives may be built up in joy and peace, we pray:

For the gift of compassion that we may carry on Christ's mission to those who suffer, we pray:

For the gift of wisdom that enables to us to make sound and prudent choices in life, we pray:

For the gift of patience that we may draw the strength to live with all that is incomplete, we pray:

For the gift of humility that frees us to rely on God's grace and power, we pray:

For the gift of prayer that we may be sustained on the riches of Christ, we pray:

For the gift of peace that we may be a healing presence to others, we pray:

For the gift of eternal life that we may thank God face to face for every blessing, we pray:

Presider: Loving God, we ask that you bestow on us gifts in keeping with the glory of Christ. Hear our prayers which we place before you through Christ, our compassionate Savior.

+ Since these petitions may be used for each cycle of readings, extra intercessions have been inserted. It is recommended that no more than six intercessions be used.

Christ the King (A, B, and C)

Presider: In baptism we were claimed for the reign of heaven. Let us pray to live as a people of the new creation where Christ reigns.

Petition Leader: Our prayer response is: **"Christ, keep us faithful to you."**

Mindful that Christ is the eternal high priest of the good things to come, may we keep in mind our call to be a priestly people praising God's mercy. We pray:

Remembering that Christ is the faithful witness of God's enduring love, may we be faithful witnesses of God's compassion for the poor, sick, and needy of our time. We pray:

Rejoicing that Christ has reconciled all things to God through his cross, may we give witness to the gospel of peace through nonviolent living. We pray:

Longing in hope for the new creation where every tear will be wiped away, may we use our voices to encourage world leaders to secure justice for the oppressed. We pray:

Remembering that God's covenant with David is fulfilled in Christ, may all the nations of the earth be gathered into the heavenly Jerusalem on the last day. We pray:

Believing that Christ is the judge of the living and the dead, may we be consoled that in Christ the faithful departed find abundant redemption. (In particular we entrust to Christ _____.) We pray:

Presider: Christ, Alpha and Omega, hear us invoking your help. Sustain us in grace that we may enter your reign when all is complete, for you live and reign forever and ever.

Presentation of the Lord (A, B, and C)

February 2

Presider: Let us invoke the Spirit of light that we may be filled with praise for God and love for our neighbor.

Petition Leader: Our response is, **"Spirit of Jesus, fill us with light."**

Simeon awaited the consolation of Israel. May all who live justly and reverently experience God's consoling love manifested in Word and Spirit. We pray:

Simeon took the child in his arms and praised God. May all who embrace Christ as the glory of Israel be filled with the Spirit of praise. We pray:

Simeon beheld the light of God's salvation enfleshed in the child Jesus. May all who feast on the body and blood of Christ be filled with the light of love. We pray:

Simeon recognized that God's redeeming love was a gift to Gentiles and Jews. May the universal church continue the ecumenical work of uniting all Christians in a single living temple of praise. We pray:

Simeon announced to Mary that Jesus would be a sign to be opposed. May we not be discouraged when there is public opposition to the gospel of peace. We pray:

Simeon prayed to be dismissed in peace. May the dead who have believed in Christ see eternal light. We pray:

Anna, a woman of fasting and prayer, publicly proclaimed Christ. May the church increasingly encourage the prophetic gifts of women and welcome their fuller participation in church ministries. We pray:

Presider: God of all, you give us Christ, the messenger of your covenant, to be our light. May we be purified by the light of Christ's word and be filled with your Spirit. Grant our prayer through Christ, our Savior and brother.

Annunciation of the Lord (A, B, and C)

March 25

Presider: In Christ, the Word-Made-Flesh, God's kindness is forever established among the children of earth. Let us pray that our fidelity to Christ's word will establish us forever in heaven.

Petition Leader: Our response is, **"Christ Emmanuel, hear our prayer."**

In the Word-Made-Flesh, our humanity has been embraced by God; may we strive with loving hearts to always embrace the divine will. We pray:

In the Word-Made-Flesh, God's steadfast love has been enfleshed; may we enflesh Christ's mercy to those who suffer in body, mind, and spirit. We pray:

In the Word-Made-Flesh, sinners are reconciled to God; may our baptismal consecration to Christ lead others to the wellspring of mercy. We pray:

In the Word-Made-Flesh, the glory of God is shown among us; may we constantly seek to renew all humanity by the grace and peace of the Holy Spirit. We pray:

In the Word-Made-Flesh, a new covenant has been established for all peoples; may our covenant with Christ inspire us to work for greater healing among enemies. We pray:

In the Word-Made-Flesh, we are shown the way to eternal joy; may our communion in the body and blood of Christ lead us to everlasting life. We pray:

Presider: Loving God, whose mercy is everlasting, in the incarnation of your Eternal Word humanity has been given a lasting hope. Hear our prayers and bless our lives that they may faithfully reflect the mystery of your presence among us, through Christ, our Lord.

Transfiguration of the Lord (A, B, and C)

August 6

Presider: Let us pray.

Petition Leader: Today we pray: **"May all praise your glory, O Christ."**

For those who envision a creation filled with enduring peace born of your Spirit; sustain us by your Word until your glory fills creation. We pray:

For those who await the morning star of unfailing justice; sustain us in hope until your reign is complete. We pray:

For those whose prophetic lives give witness to your enduring reign of love; sustain us by your Spirit until God is all in all. We pray:

For those whom you call to intimacy with yourself through contemplative and mystical prayer; sustain us with the richest spiritual gifts in keeping with your splendor. We pray:

For those who seek to discern your voice and fulfill your will; sustain us in faith until your eternal glory is fully revealed. We pray:

For those who served you with reverence during their earthly pilgrimage; sustain all the dead by the power of your resurrection. We pray:

Presider: God of glory and majesty, you revealed your choicest love in Christ. Help us to listen to your Beloved, in whose name we pray, that we may be sustained by the words of everlasting life.

Triumph of the Cross (A, B, and C)

September 14

Presider: Lifted up on the cross, Christ has become the source of eternal life. Let us invoke the saving power of the risen Savior.

Petition Leader: Our prayer response is: **"Redeemer of the world, hear us."**

May the power of your cross bring solace and comfort to all whose lives are marked with the cross of poverty and abuse. We ask in faith:

May the power of your cross bring healing to families torn apart by dissension, addictions, and disregard for others' emotional needs. We ask in faith:

May the power of your cross restore life to the sick who call out to you for healing. We ask in faith:

May the power of your cross uphold those who are afflicted with depression and despair and who contemplate suicide. We ask in faith:

May the power of your cross be the source of spiritual vitality for all vowed religious and clergy. We ask in faith:

May the power of your cross sustain us in our passion for justice and mercy. We ask in faith:

May the power of your cross overflow your risen life to all our beloved dead. We ask in faith:

Presider: Savior of the world, in your dying and rising we are set free. Hear our prayers, and through the power of your cross bring us to the fullness of life in God's presence, where you live and reign forever and ever.

Holy Days

Immaculate Conception (A, B, and C)

December 8

Presider: Mary is the chosen daughter of Israel through whom God sent the Promise of Ages, Jesus Christ. May our voices be one with hers as we pray to Christ.

Petition Leader: Our prayer response is, **"Jesus, fill us with good things."**

O Christ, we rejoice in you in union with Mary, the vessel of honor. May your church be filled with the Spirit of all grace and peace. We pray:

O Light of Nations, we rejoice with Mary, the cause of our joy. Strengthen us to place our lives in humble service of the reign of heaven. We pray:

O Descendant of David, we praise you together with Mary, the ark of the Covenant. Guide your brothers and sisters as we carry your gospel of compassion to those who suffer in body, mind, and spirit. We pray:

O long awaited Messiah, we proclaim your mercy with Mary, conceived without original sin. Renew the world in holiness that all will be well prepared to receive you when you come again. We pray:

O Alpha and Omega, with Mary, the gate of heaven, we long for the day of salvation. Console the dying, comfort those who mourn, and reveal the light of eternity to all who died trusting in your love. We pray:

Presider: Revealing God, you have given us Jesus Christ to make us a new creation and Mary, his Mother, to be our model of faith. Help us to remain faithful to our calling that we may praise your glory in her company. We ask this in the name of Jesus, our Savior.

Mary, Mother of God (A, B, and C)

Day of Prayer for World Peace   January 1

Presider: Let us pray that the light of Christ's peace will shine throughout the world.

[Alternative invitation to prayer for the years 2000 and 2001]:

As the world welcomes this new millennium let us pray that the light of Christ's peace will bless all peoples.

Petition Leader: Our response today is, **"Savior of the world, give us your peace."**

For the church throughout the world; may its faith and hope serve as a beacon of light for the good of every nation, race, and creed. As we rejoice in your birth, we ask:

For Pope *[name]*, Catholic bishops, and all religious leaders of the Orthodox and Protestant churches; may your Spirit guide them to greater unity. As we rejoice in your birth, we ask:

For persons who address God by many different names; may the one Spirit of love and light uphold the spiritual good in all faith traditions. As we rejoice in your birth, we ask:

For world leaders and organizations that promote harmony among nations; may they be filled with your wisdom as they work to secure the common good. As we rejoice in your birth, we ask:

For our families and all who welcome this (new year/new millennium); may our homes be filled with health and happiness. As we rejoice in your birth, we ask:

For those who are enemies and cause for human suffering; may persons and groups that thwart world peace be healed of their hatred and violence. As we rejoice in your birth, we ask:

For the economically poor of the world, for all oppressed peoples, and for those deprived of their human rights; may the works of justice bring peace and freedom to every individual. As we rejoice in your birth, we ask:

Presider: God our Creator and Redeemer, in the fullness of time you entered human history through the incarnation of Christ. Hear our prayers, and by your Spirit help us to enflesh the gospel of peace we celebrate. Grant our prayers through Jesus Christ, our Savior and brother.

Assumption of Mary (A, B, and C)

August 15

Presider: Confident that Mary intercedes with the church, let us pray to be faithful to the Word that brings us eternal life.

Petition Leader: Our prayer response is, **"Lord, fill us with your love."**

Mary's being rejoices in the saving power of God. May the Spirit of her son inspire the church's praise of God's endless mercy. We pray:

Mary showed complete fidelity to the word of God and became blessed among women. May our fidelity to the gospel fill us with every spiritual blessing. We pray:

Mary hastened into the hill country to be with her kinswoman, Elizabeth. May we hasten into the hill country of human need to assist our brothers and sisters in Christ. We pray:

Mary uses her voice in the reign of God to intercede for us. May we use our voices in this realm to advocate justice for the poor. We pray:

Many people are prevented from knowing their blessedness because of mistreatment and abuse. May we use our gifts to help others affirm their dignity and self-worth. We pray:

Every day the forces of death strike at life. May we, who have been clothed in the splendor of God's Spirit, be ardent witnesses to the sanctity of all life. We pray:

Christ has been given full authority in heaven and earth. May the power of his resurrection bring us to life when our earthly journey is complete. We pray:

Presider: God our Savior, with Mary we praise the greatness of your love that sanctifies all creation. Receive our prayers and uphold your servant church in the power of your Spirit. We ask this through Jesus, our Redeemer, who lives and reigns with you and the Holy Spirit, one God forever and ever.

All Saints (A, B, and C)

November 1

Presider: Let us call forth the Holy Spirit that, like the saints, we might be filled with the light of faith and love.

Petition Leader: Our prayer response is: **"Spirit of God, dwell with us."**

May the Holy Spirit fill us with a personal love for God whom we are called to love above all else. We ask in faith:

May the Spirit of truth kindle in our hearts a passion for mercy that we may rejoice in God's mercy on our day of need. We ask in faith:

May the Spirit who raised Jesus from the dead restore life to those who have abandoned faith in Christ. We ask in faith:

May the Comforter stir in us a zeal for justice that renews the face of the earth. We ask in faith:

May the Spirit, our Counselor, be with our youth that their lives will reflect the light of Christ. We ask in faith:

May the Spirit of all grace and peace uphold those who suffer for their commitment to Christ and the gospel of life. We ask in faith:

May the Spirit who sanctified the lives of the saints bring our beloved dead into the reign of light. We ask in faith:

Presider: God of compassion, you have shared the victory of Christ with the saints. Hear our prayers for your Spirit that our lives will be rooted in love and make us worthy to share the joy of the saints. We ask this in Jesus' name.

All Souls (A, B, and C)

November 2

Presider: The light of Christ's resurrection reveals the immensity of God's mercy. Let us pray that our faith in God's mercy and love be fortified.

Petition Leader: Our response is: **"God of the living and the dead, uphold us."**

When we grieve the loss of those we love, we ask:

When we invoke the saving death of Christ for any who are still deprived of your eternal light, we ask:

When we call on your mercy for those who have died without the consolation of baptism, we ask:

When death is caused by human malice and anger robs us of peace, we ask:

When our faith in your providential care is challenged, we ask:

When terminal illness signals that our earthly pilgrimage is coming to an end, we ask:

When our only consolation is the hope of seeing you face to face, we ask:

Presider: God, rich in compassion, hear our prayers for those who have died. Sustain your pilgrim people in the hope that your promise of mercy reaches all humanity. We ask this through Christ Jesus, the first-born of all the dead.

Sundays in
Ordinary Time

Second Sunday in Ordinary Time (A)

Presider: Let us call on the name of Christ asking for grace and peace.

Petition Leader: Our response is, **"Christ Jesus, hear our prayer."**

For the church consecrated for service on behalf of the reign of heaven; may it witness to Christ, the Lamb of God, as the source of universal salvation. We pray:

For those who help others rebuild lives devastated by tragedy and disaster; may the kindness and goodwill of so many be an inspiration to all. We pray:

For engaged couples; may the Spirit guide all who are preparing for the sacrament of marriage. We pray:

For the elderly and physically disabled who are homebound by winter's ice and snow; may their needs not be forgotten by relatives and friends. We pray:

For police officers and firefighters; may those who serve to protect citizens from harm be distinguished for their personal dedication. We pray:

For developmentally disadvantaged persons; may the Spirit of God provide them with every special grace and blessing. We pray:

For any personal needs and intentions, let us now pray quietly [pause for sufficient reflection]. We pray:

Presider: Gracious God, receive our prayers and help us to live as your holy people. We ask this in Jesus' name.

Second Sunday in Ordinary Time (B)

Presider: The world is filled with spiritual seekers, and the church itself is called to seek Christ constantly. Let us pray that the Spirit will guide us to the divine presence.

Petition Leader: Our response today is, **"Lord, help us to seek and find you."**

As John the Baptist pointed out the Lamb of God to his disciples, so may we be attentive to the prophetic voices that reveal Christ's presence. We pray:

As the Most High called Samuel, so may our youth be responsive to the call of Christ in the Spirit. We pray:

As Eli understood the movements of God in the life of Samuel, so may those who serve as spiritual directors and pastoral counselors be blessed with wisdom. We pray:

As Andrew brought his brother to Christ, so may we use our faith to bring our sisters and brothers to discipleship with the world's Redeemer. We pray:

As our bodies are temples of the sacred, may Christians be forerunners in promoting physical and moral integrity for all people as a witness to Christ. We pray:

As Jesus invited the disciples to "come and see," so may the Spirit place in our hearts the desire for intimacy with the God of our salvation. We pray:

As Jesus welcomed these first disciples, so may the compassionate Savior welcome into the reign of heaven all who have died hoping to see God (especially _____). We pray:

Presider: Kind and loving God, you revealed your presence among us in Christ, our Savior. Receive our prayers and bless all people with spiritual gifts that lead to the fullness of life in Christ. We pray in the name of the Lamb of God.

Second Sunday in Ordinary Time (C)

Presider: Through the Spirit's gift of prayer let us intercede for the church and the world.

Petition Leader: Our response is: **"God in heaven, hear us."**

That the grace of the Holy Spirit will enable church leaders and theologians to discern God speaking through the signs of our times, we pray:

That we will affirm our faith community as one of the Spirit's gifts and be of service to it through ordained and lay ministries or religious life, we pray:

That the Spirit's gifts of wisdom and knowledge will be with all who are facing career choices, particularly graduating students, we pray:

That the seriously ill will be helped by the Spirit's gift of right judgment as they face medical treatment and care choices, we pray:

That through our celebration of eucharist the transforming love of the Spirit will draw us into deeper bonds of unity and peace, we pray:

That the dead will be received into the wedding feast of heaven (particularly _____), we pray:

Presider: God, hear our prayers and accomplish in us your saving will through the working of the Holy Spirit. Grant this through Christ, our Lord.

Third Sunday in Ordinary Time (A)

Presider: Let us pray that the light of Christ will help us overcome any darkness that surrounds us.

Petition Leader: Our prayer response is, **"Christ, be our light."**

For Christian leaders and theologians as they work to heal divisions among Christians, we pray:

For lay missionary couples who set aside personal security and profit to proclaim the good news, we pray:

For medical personnel who must make treatment and care decisions for the critically ill, especially in emergency circumstances, we pray:

For guidance counselors, educators, and social workers who companion youth in times of doubt, frustration, and uncertainty, we pray:

For bereavement counselors and funeral directors as they walk with others in the darkness of grief, we pray:

For persons whose lives are adversely affected by racism, especially in housing and real estate, we pray:

Presider: Loving God, in so many ways you invite us to spread the light of Christ. Receive our prayers, and by the Holy Spirit help us to continue to follow the One who is Light from Light, Jesus Christ.

Third Sunday in Ordinary Time (B)

Presider: The Word of Life calls the world to conversion for the sake of God's reign. Let us invoke the transforming grace of the Spirit that we may take to heart the good news we have heard.

Petition Leader: After each petition will be a moment for silent prayer. [Leader, please allow for a sufficient pause after each petition.]

In their encounter with the prophetic call of Jonah, the people of Nineveh repented. May we take to heart the prophetic voices that call us away from the evil of violence.

Through the instruction of the apostle Paul, Christians were taught to be far-sighted. May the wisdom of God help us not to lose sight of our eternal destiny in Christ.

Our daily affairs can be all-consuming. May we constantly make room in our lives for daily prayer and reflection on God's saving love.

The city of Nineveh entered into a fast that brought forth God's mercy. May all citizens work to improve the quality of life for others out of love for God.

The call of Christ came to the disciples in the midst of their employment. May our workplaces hold opportunities for deepening our Christian vocation.

The disciples abandoned their livelihood and family ties to follow Christ. May our career goals and personal relationships not impede us from living the gospel.

Presider: God of mercy, your word calls us constantly to abandon sin. Your Living Word, Jesus Christ, called the disciples to abandon their nets. Help us to be free from all that stands in the way of our fulfilling your will. Grant our prayers in Jesus' name.

Third Sunday in Ordinary Time (C)

Presider: Let us pray in the strength of our faith, rejoicing that God's saving Word is in our midst.

Petition Leader: Our response is, **"Hear our prayer, gracious God."**

God gives us many material blessings to enjoy. We pray for the gift of generosity that we may share our blessings with those who have less. So we ask:

Negative attitudes diminish our bonds of unity. We pray to grow in mutual respect and to celebrate the gifts of the Spirit that surround us. So we ask:

Jesus came in the Spirit's power to reveal the compassion of God. We pray that the works of mercy will flourish among us. So we ask:

Many people are trapped by materialism. We pray that Christians will cultivate lifestyles built on simplicity, respect for natural resources, and principles of justice. So we ask:

The people rejoiced in hearing the word of God. We pray that the Spirit will deepen our love for sacred scripture. So we ask:

Ezra proclaimed that the sabbath was holy to the Most High. May we use the Lord's day for praising God, respecting the body's need for rest, and looking in on neighbors in need. So we ask:

Presider: God of mercy, your Living Word prompts our prayer and raises our hearts to ask for your help. Keep us joyful in spirit, united in faith, and generous in our love. Grant this in Jesus' name.

Fourth Sunday in Ordinary Time (A)

Presider: Let us pray to live the gospel.

Petition Leader: Our response is, **"Lord, hear our prayer."**

For the church; may the people of God constantly seek to discern the Spirit's movement and fulfill God's will. We pray:

For the world's poor and lowly; may a servant church companion all who are struggling to affirm the blessedness of their humanity. We pray:

For civic and religious organizations that provide relief services in time of catastrophe and disasters; may their work of compassion reveal God's care. We pray:

For special commissions that serve peace processes; may God's Spirit grace the efforts of negotiating teams to restore civility and harmony. We pray:

For those who grieve the loss of a loved one; may personal prayer be a rich source of strength and consolation. We pray:

For the gift of perseverance in proclaiming the gospel even when confronted with hostile opposition. We pray:

For all who have died in the peace of Christ (especially _____). We pray:

Presider: God of mercy, hear our prayers for your saving grace. May the church live the gospel it has received. We pray this through Christ, our Lord.

Fourth Sunday in Ordinary Time (B)

Presider: Let us call upon the freeing power of Christ to bring healing and new life to the world.

Petition Leader: Our prayer response today is: **"Holy One of God, have mercy!"**

May all who speak in the name of Christ, especially religious leaders, announce the prophetic word of God's peace. In faith we call out:

In all times and places may the church devote itself to the teachings of Jesus and come to know the liberating love of God. In faith we call out:

Christ rebuked the oppressive voice of evil. May Christ's power at work in us help free the world of all that still oppresses human life. In faith we call out:

Whether married or single, vowed religious or clergy, may all Christians grow in their respective dedication to the work of God's reign. In faith we call out:

Through the sacramental ministries of the church may the healing power of God restore wholeness to all who rely on God's compassion. In faith we call out:

May people of goodwill greet God with thanksgiving by reverencing the dignity of every person, since all are made in the image of the Creator. In faith we call out:

The power of death has been rebuked by Christ. May the dead who appear before Christ in the heavenly temple receive new life (especially _____). In faith we call out:

Presider: God, your saving power was revealed in our midst through your Anointed, Jesus Christ. May the anointing Spirit be with us as we call on your mercy and love in Jesus' name.

Fourth Sunday in Ordinary Time (C)

Presider: Let us pray to set our hearts on the greater gifts of faith, hope, and love.

Petition Leader: Our response is: **"God of love, bring us new life."**

For the people of God called to love God and neighbor; may the greatest of gifts be witnessed in our commitment to a life of prayer, peace, justice, and compassion. We pray:

For any who suffer from depression and emotional anxieties; may the gift of hope in God's freeing love be a source of healing. We pray:

For an increase of patience in our day-to-day relationships; may the Spirit enable us to be kind and gentle in spite of others' imperfections. We pray:

For a deepening of respect for people's dignity; may we be quick to affirm what is right by discouraging racist and sexist language and jokes. We pray:

For the grace to overcome jealousy and arrogance; may the Spirit free us to rejoice in others' gifts and to walk humbly with God. We pray:

For a maturing of Christian faith; may we take every opportunity to increase our knowledge of the Christian mysteries, of scripture and the sacraments. We pray:

Presider: God, you call us in Christ to be a holy and prophetic people. May your church be fortified by the Holy Spirit, and may the greatest of gifts flourish in us. Grant this through Christ, our Lord.

Fifth Sunday in Ordinary Time (A)

Presider: Let us pray that Christians will carry the light of the gospel throughout the world.

Petition Leader: Our response is, **"Lord of Light, bless us."**

That the faithful will find rich nourishment in the bread of God's word, we pray:

That Christians will reach out to the spiritually homeless and clothe them with gospel of Jesus Christ, we pray:

That organizations committed to providing food and shelter to those in need will find strong support and benefactors in each local community, we pray:

That all Christians might be committed to using respectful language, telling the truth, and upholding the dignity of the Divine Name, we pray:

That Christian parents will be generous in sharing the bread of moral and spiritual guidance with their children, we pray:

That all citizens of the United States will be generous in offering hospitality and welcome to immigrants, especially those fleeing oppressive circumstances, we pray:

That the Spirit will guide all who seek to relieve human misery and address its causes, we pray:

Presider: Eternal God, may your goodness be reflected in our lives. Help us to walk as a people of the light in union with Jesus, who lives and reigns forever and ever.

Fifth Sunday in Ordinary Time (B)

Presider: The presence of Jesus restored health and hope to God's people. Let us pray to live the word of Life that we may be a source of joy in the lives of others.

Petition Leader: Our prayer response today is, **"God of mercy, hear our prayer."**

In their encounter with the Living Word, the sick and oppressed found new life. May we have the courage to proclaim gospel truths that free the world by the power of God. With hope-filled joy, we ask:

Christ found strength in the power of prayer. May we be absorbed by the Spirit who can transform our lives for the sake of others. With hope-filled joy, we ask:

Christ expelled the demons that deprived people of joy. May we use our influence to address the causes that rob people of quality life. With hope-filled joy, we ask:

Christ journeyed through the villages with the good news of salvation. May we be carriers of a new vision of God's mercy in our global village. With hope-filled joy, we ask:

Graced by God to be weak for the sake of the weak, St. Paul brought others to faith. May we offer a compelling witness to the gospel in spite of our limitations. With hope-filled joy, we ask:

Every day people are searching for spiritual values and lasting peace. May spiritual seekers find in our eucharistic community a vibrant love and faith. With hope-filled joy, we ask:

Presider: Gracious God, hear our prayers and keep alive in us the joy and vitality of the gospel. Grant our prayer through your Anointed, Jesus Christ.

Fifth Sunday in Ordinary Time (C)

Presider: Let us pray to stand firm in the gospel that has been proclaimed to us through the apostles and evangelists.

Petition Leader: Our prayer response today is: **"God of glory, hear us."**

That our belief in the death and resurrection of Christ will inspire us to share our faith with unchurched persons, we pray:

That our hearts will be touched by the Spirit's fire, inspiring us to carry on Christ's mission of mercy, we pray:

That our praise of God, whose glory fills the earth, will move us to be respectful of creation, its natural resources and ecology, we pray:

That all who work to discover cures and immunizations for fatal diseases will be blessed in their work, we pray:

That newly arrived immigrants will find warm welcome in our neighborhoods and parishes, we pray:

That Christian realtors will hold fast to fair housing and avoid all forms of discrimination in their businesses, we pray:

That all the dead will behold the risen Christ (especially _____), we pray:

Presider: Holy and eternal God, you have chosen us in Christ to be your faithful people. Through our prayers may your Spirit rest in our hearts and bring us your help. We ask this in Jesus' name.

Sixth Sunday in Ordinary Time (A)

Presider: Let us call forth Wisdom that we may attain spiritual maturity.

Petition Leader: Our response is, **"Pour forth your Spirit, O God."**

Send us Wisdom, the attendant at your throne, that we will recognize the path that leads to life. We pray:

Send us Wisdom's purity that we may safeguard our personal integrity at all times. We pray:

Send us Wisdom that by her intelligence we may pursue the truth that sets us free. We pray:

Send us Wisdom that like her we may love what is good and detest what is evil. We pray:

Send Wisdom's light to all who serve in judicial roles or on juries, or who are called to testify in trials, that honesty and truth will prevail at all times. We pray:

Send Wisdom's kindliness to all husbands and wives, that they may live in fidelity and mutual respect. We pray:

Presider: God of glory, in the power of your Spirit, Christ proclaimed your law of love in the fullness of Wisdom. Send us your Spirit that we may share the riches of Christ and come to eternal splendor. We ask this in Jesus' name.

Sixth Sunday in Ordinary Time (B)

Presider: Let us pray to do all for the glory of God whether at home, in school, or in our workplaces.

Petition Leader: Our prayer response today is, **"In your kindness, hear us."**

May our lives be enriched by the Spirit of God that we may live as the compassionate Christ. In faith we ask God:

May human efforts to promote quality health care to persons with contagious diseases and alienating illnesses find strong support among our country's leaders. In faith we ask God:

May the example of Jesus free Christians from any fear of providing quality care and friendship to persons who are HIV-positive or dying from AIDS. In faith we ask God:

May we imitate St. Paul, who out of love for Christ set aside all self-seeking and arrogance. In faith we ask God:

May our Christian witness to God's inclusive love provide encouragement to persons who feel unloved and unwanted. In faith we ask God:

May the dead who appear before Christ blemished by sin find mercy and healing. In faith we ask God:

Presider: How wonderful is your love, gracious God! How immense your mercies! Your Word of Life gives us hope and inspires us to call on your kindness in the name of Christ, who lives and reigns with you and the Holy Spirit forever.

Sixth Sunday in Ordinary Time (C)

Presider: Faith in the resurrection of Christ calls us to be servants of the good news. Let us entrust our vocation to God's mercy and love.

Petition Leader: Our prayer response is: **"Increase our faith, O God."**

For a deepening of trust in God's sustaining love as we age and our physical energy diminishes, we pray:

For the gift of a vibrant prayer life that we may draw strength from the Spirit in times of personal trial and crisis, we pray:

For the grace to place spiritual well-being and moral goodness above material success and power, we pray:

For the ability to care deeply for all who are burdened by poverty, physical suffering, and lack of food, especially the homeless, we pray:

For the light of faith to come as gift to those who see Jesus only as a moral teacher, we pray:

For the blessing of good humor that we may bring laughter and joy to our homes and workplaces at no one's expense, we pray:

Presider: God and Abba of Jesus, hear our prayers and grant that the gift of your life may flourish in us. We pray in Jesus' name.

Seventh Sunday in Ordinary Time (A)

Presider: Let us invoke God to preserve us in the grace and peace of Christ.

Petition Leader: Our prayer response is, **"Give us your love and grace, Lord."**

Through the Spirit's presence may the church live in fullness the saving mystery of Jesus Christ. We pray:

Through the Spirit's power may our love for the word of God intensify. We pray:

Through the Spirit of holiness may all Christians strive for forgiveness in hurting relationships. We pray:

Through the grace of the Spirit may we build inclusive communities of compassion in keeping with the love of Christ. We pray:

Through the Creator Spirit may we cherish the earth and all its resources. We pray:

Through the Spirit who raised Jesus from the dead, may our dead rise to eternal life (especially _____). We pray:

Presider: Compassionate God, hear our prayers, and by the grace of the Spirit may the love and wisdom of Christ dwell in us. We ask this in Jesus' name.

Seventh Sunday in Ordinary Time (B)

Presider: Sealed in Christ through the Holy Spirit we are united to the mystery of God's saving work. Let us pray to hold firm to our sacred calling.

Petition Leader: Our prayer response is: **"God, be our help!"**

Proclaiming forgiveness of sin, Christ broke new ground for compassionate living. May Christians cultivate the healing power of forgiveness in all situations. We pray:

Human beings created a barrier to those trying to reach Jesus. May the Spirit enlighten us to the ways in which human behaviors create barriers to the sacred. We pray:

Acting in faith, the paralytic's friends dismantled the roof to reach Jesus. May we work to dismantle oppressive structures that keep people paralyzed. We pray:

The witnesses to the paralytic's healing were filled with praise. May we give God glory when we see blessings come to others in Christ's name. We pray:

Through the prophet Isaiah we are taught that God does not hold on to our sins. May we not keep a list of the faults and failings of others. We pray:

In Christ the new way promised by God is fulfilled. May the dead who followed the way of love stand before God in fullness of joy (especially_____). We pray:

Presider: God, your promises have come to pass in Christ. In the Savior's name hear our prayers and strengthen our baptismal promise to live as your people forever.

Seventh Sunday in Ordinary Time (C)

Presider: Our call to discipleship with Christ invites us to journey in mercy. Let us pray that compassion will be the hallmark of the church (as the new millennium dawns/in our time).

Petition Leader: In faith let us call out, **"Compassionate God, hear our prayer."**

Christ Jesus, protect us from people of violence. In turn, may we work to transform the culture of death that surrounds us. In your name we ask:

Christ, you teach us to love our enemies. May our gift of faith inspire us always to be healers where injury exists. In your name we ask:

Savior, you desire that we be pure of heart. May we discourage entertainment, literature, and recreation that glorify violence in any form. In your name we ask:

Christ crucified, you did not condemn the sinner. May our belief in the power of forgiveness make us advocates for life, not death penalties. In your name we ask:

Light of the World, you call us to the higher virtues. May our discipleship influence our conduct in business, political, and professional undertakings. In your name we ask:

Bread of Life, we gather at table to celebrate your loving kindness. May our gratitude show itself in our kindness and consideration for others. In your name we ask:

Presider: God, not according to our sins do you respond to us, but according to your mercy. In the greatness of your love hear our prayers and help us to put into action the gospel of life we have heard. We ask this in the name of your servant and our Savior, Jesus Christ.

Eighth Sunday in Ordinary Time (A)

Presider: Let us turn to God and ask for the faith to trust Divine Providence.

Petition Leader: Our response is, **"Increase our faith, O God."**

By God's grace may we come to believe in the love God has for us. We pray:

By the gift of hope may those who feel desolate be renewed in spirit. We pray:

By the power of God's word may we live secure in peace. We pray:

By the wisdom of God may a servant church help the world's wealthy rise above self-centered materialism. We pray:

By the strength of the Holy Spirit may we address the life and death issues that affect the economically poor of the world. We pray:

By the example of Christ may all who are fed at the table of life pursue the way of self-giving love. We pray:

Presider: God, indeed you never forget us, and you listen attentively to your people's prayer. In your kindness and love help us to grow in the ways of faith. We ask this in Jesus' name.

Eighth Sunday in Ordinary Time (B)

Presider: The wedding feast of heaven has begun in Jesus. Let us ask the espousing Spirit of God to enliven in us the covenant of new life.

Petition Leader: Our prayer response today is, **"Spirit of God, give us life."**

In the death of God's Anointed, creation has been freed from its slavery to sin; may church leaders continue to labor for human freedom. Confidently we ask:

In the resurrection of Jesus heaven has been wedded to earth; may all peoples come to know the one true God who redeems us in Christ. Confidently we ask:

In the pentecost the Spirit roused the disciples to boldly proclaim the gospel; may the same Spirit make all legislators advocates for the poor. Confidently we ask:

In baptism we have been claimed for the reign of heaven; may we live as a priestly people renewing the world in Christ's peace. Confidently we ask:

In our celebration of eucharist the Spirit unites the church at one table; may the new wine we share as Christ's covenant fortify in us the gift of love. Confidently we ask:

In death our earthly pilgrimage is ended; may our deceased loved ones come to know God face to face (especially _____). Confidently we ask:

Presider: Redeeming God, through the gift of your Spirit we come to life in Christ. May we cling to the new life you have placed in our hearts. Grant our prayer in Jesus' name.

Eighth Sunday in Ordinary Time (C)

Presider: Let us pray that our faith will be fruitful to God's honor and glory.

Petition Leader: Our response is: **"Just God, show us your love."**

That our efforts to improve the quality of life for all will find blessing with God, we pray:

That the ministry of health care and social service professionals will show forth God's care for the poor, the sick, and the elderly, we pray:

That we will live in accord with our supernatural destiny in Christ, we pray:

That our words and speech will be kind and encouraging rather than harsh or critical, we pray:

That we will walk humbly with God, mindful of our imperfections, we pray:

That the dead will be clothed with immortality in Christ (especially _____), we pray:

Let us now pray quietly for any personal needs and intentions [pause for sufficient reflection]. We pray:

Presider: Loving God, accept the prayers of our community and those in the quiet of our hearts, through Christ, our Lord.

Ninth Sunday in Ordinary Time (A)

Presider: Let us pray.

Petition Leader: Our response today is, **"God in heaven, hear us."**

For the grace to build our lives on God's unfailing word rather than on the unstable foundations of wealth and power, we pray:

For a maturing of Christian discipleship that all believers will strive with sincere hearts to put the gospel into practice, we pray:

For the light of faith to come to all people so that the human race may rejoice in the gift of salvation, we pray:

For catechists and educators as they work to help youth build lives on the rock of redemption, who is Jesus Christ, we pray:

For all who have died trusting in God's mercy and love (particularly _____), we pray:

Presider: Saving God, hear our prayers and help us to live as a faith-filled people. We pray in Jesus' name.

Ninth Sunday in Ordinary Time (B)

Presider: Let us pray that all the world may come to know the light of God's unconditional love.

Petition Leader: Our prayer response today is, **"Creating God, hear us."**

God created the sabbath that all people may rest from their labors. May we respect the body's need for rest and leisure. We pray:

God freed the Israelites from the hands of their slave-drivers. May state and national leaders assure fair labor practices and equal wages for all workers. We pray:

Christ freed humanity from its slavery to religious legalisms. May the freeing Spirit enable Christian communities to be havens of compassion. We pray:

Our faith calls us to make the glory of Christ known to all peoples. May the anointing Spirit raise up servants of the gospel who will renew human hopes. We pray:

Jesus encountered minds closed to the healing power of God's love. May frustration and opposition not deter the church from its mission of mercy. We pray:

We are beset by weakness, doubt, and suffering. May persons who share intimately in the passion of Jesus be sustained by the consoling Spirit. We pray:

Presider: God, you have ordered all things to our benefit, even the sabbath. Hear our prayers and continue to free us to do good in the name of Christ. We ask this in the Savior's name.

Ninth Sunday in Ordinary Time (C)

Presider: The centurion's faith won favor with Christ. Let us implore God's favor for the health and life of our world.

Petition Leader: Our prayer response is: **"God, in your mercy, hear us."**

We summon your Spirit of unity to fortify the gospel of peace and reconciliation among the churches. May the oneness of the body of Christ be fully restored. In faith we pray:

We intercede for people of goodwill who are not members of the body of Christ. May your Spirit grace the hearts of all who sincerely seek the fullness of your truth and love. In faith we pray:

We ask that your Spirit of loving kindness be poured out on nations torn apart by civil wars and rivalries. May cooperation replace competition, and compassion replace cruelty. In faith we pray:

We ask for the gift of intercessory prayer so as to companion those who desire healing. By your Spirit praying in us may well-being and health come to those most in need. In faith we pray:

We call upon your fidelity to the covenant made with our ancestors in faith. May your promise of mercy fulfilled in Christ raise the dead to eternal life (especially _____). In faith we pray:

Presider: Gracious God, receive our prayers and grant that your kindness to all people may endure among us. We ask this through Jesus, our Savior.

Tenth Sunday in Ordinary Time (A)

Presider: Let us pray to be strengthened in faith that our lives will glorify God.

Petition Leader: Our prayer response is, **"God, in your kindness, hear us."**

Matthew brought his friends together to meet Jesus. As disciples of a merciful Redeemer may we bring others to Christ. We pray:

Jesus dined with tax collectors and sinners. As sharers in the messianic meal may we continue to work toward greater table unity among Christians. We pray:

Jesus fed the people the word of mercy. As people who rejoice in God's word may we follow the way of compassionate service. We pray:

Jesus calls forth our love. As a servant church may Pope *[name]*, the bishops, and clergy receive with joy the Spirit's gifts dispersed throughout the faithful. We pray:

Jesus was raised up for our salvation. As believers in the resurrection may God give eternal life to all the dead (particularly _____). We pray:

Presider: God of all creation, in faith we call out to you. In your goodness hear our prayers through Christ, our peace and reconciliation now and forever.

Tenth Sunday in Ordinary Time (B)

Presider: Let us intercede with the God of mercy to bring healing and increased peace to our world.

Petition Leader: Our prayer response is: **"In your kindness, hear us, O God!"**

As Christian leaders strive to discern the movements of your Spirit in a world often torn apart by violence and disharmony, sustain your church in wisdom. We pray:

As societies work to deepen mutual respect among peoples, give all citizens the courage to dismantle the tragedies of racism, sexism, and abuse of creation. We pray:

As medical and health care professionals strive to ease the burden of pain for the terminally ill, may they be instruments of your compassion. We pray:

As we intercede on behalf of persons who have lost heart and are burdened by despair, lavish abundant grace on any who are suicidal, especially youth. We pray:

As we discern peaceable ways to respond to false accusations and hostility in our daily lives, may your Word and Spirit help us to bear wrongs patiently. We pray:

As we fix our sight on the unseen beauty of the reign of heaven, may we abide in the hope that Christ will acknowledge the dead as his sisters and brothers (especially _____). We pray:

Presider: Redeeming God, may we not lose heart when the forces of evil and death touch our lives. By your Spirit inspire us to draw strength through prayer and find comfort in the victory of Christ, who lives and reigns with you and the Holy Spirit, one God forever and ever.

Tenth Sunday in Ordinary Time (C)

Presider: Elijah's prayer restored life to the dead child. Let our prayers invoke the saving power of Christ for the life of the world.

Petition Leader: Our response is: **"Spirit, Giver of Life, be with us!"**

Send forth your Spirit of wisdom upon the church's many educational ministries and institutions. We pray:

Send forth your Spirit of compassion upon Catholic health care ministries, hospitals, and personnel. We pray:

Send forth your Spirit of joy into all homes and marriages. We pray:

Send forth your Spirit of good counsel to those discerning vocations to the ordained ministries and religious life. We pray:

Send forth your Spirit of healing to those who are sick and in a period of recovery. We pray:

Send forth your Spirit of fortitude to those whose lives are marked by heavy crosses, especially families of missing persons. We pray:

Send forth your Spirit of Life that the dead may rise to everlasting peace. We pray:

Presider: Loving God, Christ came in the power of the Spirit to restore our lives. Hear our prayers, and by the Spirit's presence keep us alive in Christ, who lives and reigns forever and ever.

Eleventh Sunday in Ordinary Time (A)

Presider: God's love for us is proven in the death of Jesus. Let us pray to live by the Spirit of love and reconciliation.

Petition Leader: Our prayer response today is, **"Compassionate God, pour out your grace."**

We invoke the Holy Spirit to empower all servants of the gospel to reach out with tenderness to those who suffer from doubts of faith. We lift our hearts and ask:

We implore God to move with power over the hearts and minds of all who are enemies to the gospel of life. We lift our hearts and ask:

We ask for the Spirit of peace and reconciliation to bless our national and state leaders so that justice will flourish for all citizens. We lift our hearts and ask:

We pray the Holy Spirit to impart to all Christians the gift of generosity that we may share our material blessings with those who have less. We lift our hearts and ask:

We entrust to God's grace those who work with homeless and runaway youth and persons in halfway houses and addiction rehabilitation centers. We lift our hearts and ask:

We call upon the Paraclete, parent of the poor, to raise up missionaries who will minister God's consoling love to countries devastated by poverty and war. We lift our hearts and ask:

We ask the God of tender mercies to bear up those who are suicidal because of loneliness or physical and emotional suffering. We lift our hearts and ask:

Presider: God, whose compassion is everlasting, Christ has called us to carry on his mission of mercy. Hear our prayers for your Spirit that we may respond in faith and love to the gospel of your Son, who lives and reigns forever and ever.

Eleventh Sunday in Ordinary Time (B)

Presider: Mindful that it is God's loving power alone that brings forth the reign of heaven, let us pray for a deepening of hope in its promise.

Petition Leader: Our prayer response today is, **"God, our hope, hear us."**

For the church as it contemplates the wonder of God's reign; may the words of Christ draw forth its deepest longings for all that remains unseen. Trusting in God's love we pray:

For the nations of the world as they move toward the future; may human aspirations for a peaceable world be built on enduring spiritual truths. Trusting in God's love we pray:

For societies ravaged by oppression, war, and poverty; may these tragedies that diminish human hopes be addressed in light of God's healing power. Trusting in God's love we pray:

For all who desire union with God; may the spiritual goodness in all faith traditions come to perfection in the divine presence. Trusting in God's love we pray:

For persons whose vision of the new heavens has grown dim; may the Spirit rekindle the light of faith in the gospel's promise. Trusting in God's love we pray:

For religious groups oppressed by prophets and visionaries of doom; may the Spirit lead sincere believers to the truth that God redeems all through love. Trusting in God's love we pray:

Presider: God, ever gracious and kind, our hope is in your lasting goodness. Sustain our spirit through the word of redemption, Jesus Christ, who lives and reigns with you and the Holy Spirit, one God forever and ever.

Eleventh Sunday in Ordinary Time (C)

Presider: Let us pray that the life of Christ in us will grow stronger.

Petition Leader: Our response is, **"Gracious God, hear our prayer."**

May the church's ministry of reconciliation bring God's pardon and peace to those who seek forgiveness and healing in their lives. We pray:

May God's Spirit of compassion bring a change of heart to those whose violent and abusive behaviors are the cause of misery and heartbreak to others. We pray:

May any who serve in roles of leadership or public office not succumb to the lure of worldly power and affluence. We pray:

May the life of Christ we live by our common baptism encourage Christian leaders to pursue greater church unity. We pray:

May the gifts and ministry of churchwomen be warmly received in all local churches and parishes. We pray:

May the good news of salvation raise us above religious observances empty of love for God and neighbor. We pray:

Presider: Loving God, help us cling to the life of faith given to us at baptism and renewed at this table. Receive our prayers and enable our love to grow even stronger. Grant this through Christ, our Reconciliation and Peace.

Twelfth Sunday in Ordinary Time (A)

Presider: Let us pray to live in the light of God's love.

Petition Leader: Our prayer response is, **"Saving God, hear our prayer."**

God's saving love has raised a fallen world. May the church fearlessly call the world to live the beauty of graced existence in Christ. We pray:

God's mercy abounds for all in Jesus Christ. May our commitment to Christ make us instruments of God's compassion to the most needy. We pray:

God's tenderness upholds the poor. May those whose lives are threatened by violence and hatred find their lasting security in God's reliable love. We pray:

God's word assures us not to live in fear. May our faith in God's providential care deepen in times of anxiety. We pray:

God's care extends to all creation. May all people grow in their respect for the earth and nature's beauty. We pray:

God's gift of eternal life is promised to those who acknowledge Christ before humanity. May those who have died in service of the gospel be raised on the last day. We pray:

Presider: Kind and tender God, hear our prayers and sustain us in Christ, our Savior.

Twelfth Sunday in Ordinary Time (B)

Presider: Christ invited the disciples to set sail for the farther shore of God's kingdom. Let us pray that the love of Christ will be our strength for journeying in faith.

Petition Leader: Our prayer response today is, **"Uphold us in your love."**

The gospel has called us away from the old and familiar. May the Spirit sustain our hopes when we must journey through periods of spiritual darkness. We call out to Christ and ask:

In the midst of the storm Christ's word restored calm. May persons overwhelmed by violence and emotional chaos find peace in Christ's presence. We call out to Christ and ask:

The tragedies of life often spur questions of the divine goodness. May our powerlessness deepen our reliance on God's abiding care. We call out to Christ and ask:

In the baptismal waters we have died with Christ. May the Spirit continue to draw us to the newness of life which the gospel holds out. We call out to Christ and ask:

We are called to have the heart and mind of Christ. May the Spirit help us to see all people and events through the light of love. We call out to Christ and ask:

For the dead the old order has passed away. May they rejoice in the new creation that Christ attained through his death (especially _____). We call out to Christ and ask:

Presider: Redeeming God, uphold us in the love of Christ that we may venture on the wider sea that leads to the glory of your reign, where Jesus is Lord forever and ever.

Twelfth Sunday in Ordinary Time (C)

Presider: In faith let us implore God to lavish grace and peace upon all humanity.

Petition Leader: Our prayer response is: **"God, have mercy."**

In baptism we have become members of the whole Christ. May our communion with Christ draw us closer to each other without distinctions based on race or gender. We pray:

In baptism we clothed ourselves in Christ, the compassionate Redeemer. May our love clothe those who are naked and stripped of dignity. We pray:

On the cross Jesus was pierced for our offenses. May our remembrance of the death of Jesus in this meal bring us health of body and spirit. We pray:

Christ calls us to follow the way of self-giving love. May we learn the meaning of discipleship from those who live the passion. We pray:

Every day countless women and children take up the cross of poverty. May we help carry their cross through our efforts to reduce their sufferings. We pray:

Unlike others who fled from Calvary, the women remained at the foot of the cross in solidarity with their friend in his agony. May we not abandon our friends when suffering afflicts them. We pray:

Presider: God, in your mercy hear our prayers, and help us to follow the way of love that leads to your reign. We ask this through your servant and our Savior, Jesus Christ.

Thirteenth Sunday in Ordinary Time (A)

Presider: Jesus, risen from the dead, is fully alive in God. Let us pray that all may come to the fullness of life.

Petition Leader: Our prayer response today is, **"Christ, our Life, hear our prayer."**

May the new life of grace given to us in baptism be manifest in our personal commitment to do God's will. We pray:

May all who are fed at the table of God's word be inspired to feed the world with the gospel of peace. We pray:

May all who rejoice at the banquet of the Lamb be fortified to take up their cross out of love for Christ. We pray:

May all who are strengthened by the sacraments of reconciliation and healing be filled with praise for God's compassion. We pray:

May the world grow in its capacity to offer hospitality and care to others, particularly to travelers and those far from home. We pray:

May we bring a blessing wherever our travels may take us. We pray:

May the dead who pursued the gospel's way of love not want for a heavenly reward. We pray:

Presider: God in heaven, we pray to be alive for you in life and death. Hear our prayers and sustain us in your grace, through Christ, our Redeemer.

Thirteenth Sunday in Ordinary Time (B)+

Presider: Let us implore the Giver of Life to fill us with the light of Christ's love and compassion.

Petition Leader: Our prayer response today is, **"Spirit, move in power over us!"**

Come, Holy Spirit; descend upon our church and world that all peoples may uphold the sacredness of life and creation. We pray:

Come, anointing Spirit; bless our spiritual leaders, especially Pope *[name]* and our bishop, *[name]*, with your wisdom and fortitude. We pray:

Come, Parent of the poor; in your unfailing kindness sustain our sisters and brothers victimized by famine, racism, and greed. We pray:

Come, healing Spirit; renew the health and well-being of all the sick, especially infants and children. We pray:

Come, consoling Spirit; comfort parents who anguish over the health and spiritual good of their children. We pray:

Come, enlightening Spirit; teach us how to safeguard the rights and dignity of all women throughout the world. We pray:

Come, gracious Spirit; open our hearts to relieve the sufferings of others. We pray:

Come, Spirit of the living God; bring all the dead to the glory of the resurrection (especially_____). We pray:

Presider: Redeeming God, may your Holy Spirit, the Giver of Life, sustain in us the beauty and truth of your Redeeming Word, Jesus Christ, who lives and reigns forever and ever.

+ Since these petitions are styled to be a litany, the number of intercessions exceeds the customary limit. They should be proclaimed swiftly but not in a rushed or hurried manner. They accompany the readings of the day and are inspired by the pentecost sequence.

Thirteenth Sunday in Ordinary Time (C)

Presider: Jesus' mission of mercy led to Jerusalem where he took up his cross. Let us pray to be faithful to the journey Christ has called us to share.

Petition Leader: Our prayer response is, **"Jesus, show us the way."**

The church is called to follow the One who had no resting place on earth. May the Spirit keep our pilgrim hearts alive for Christ. We ask in faith:

The call to proclaim the good news required total commitment. May the grace of God free us from being dead to our baptismal vocation. We ask in faith:

The gift of the Spirit liberates humanity for service to God's reign. With the Spirit's help may all people use their freedom to build communities of care. We ask in faith:

James and John, the sons of thunder, were inclined toward destructive power. May Jesus' reprimand remind all people that violence and cruelty have no part in Christ's mission. We ask in faith:

The Teacher has shown us the path to life. May young persons who are leaving home to pursue their futures seek out the light of Christ continuously. We ask in faith:

Presider: God of perfect peace, Christ has purchased our freedom through the cross. Hear our prayers asking that we follow the way of true discipleship. Grant our prayers through Christ, our Way, our Truth, and our Life.

Fourteenth Sunday in Ordinary Time (A)

Presider: Christ invites us to be refreshed in his love. Let us entrust to the Redeemer our concerns.

Petition Leader: Our prayer response is, **"Christ, in your mercy, hear us."**

We pray that the church will be enriched with many fresh vocations to the ordained ministries, to religious life, and to lay apostolates that serve the needy. In faith we ask:

We entrust to your care poorer nations that are heavily burdened by debt; may their debtors be moved to lighten their financial obligations. In faith we ask:

We intercede on behalf of races that are wearied through all forms of discrimination; may your Spirit sustain the hopes of all who long for a just world. In faith we ask:

We place before you those whose hearts have been broken by the loss of a loved one. In faith we ask:

We ask you to renew in spirit those whose hearts have been hardened by aggression and who devalue the gift of life for themselves or others. In faith we ask:

We rely on your mercy to uphold the sick, especially those whose earthly journey is coming to a close. In faith we ask:

We entrust to you the personal needs and intentions we carry within our hearts this day. [Pause for silent reflection.] In faith we ask:

Presider: Christ, just Savior, we rejoice heartily in the tender mercy of God that is revealed in you. Hear our prayers, for all our trust is in you, who lives and reigns forever and ever.

Fourteenth Sunday in Ordinary Time (B)

Presider: Let us pray that the grace of God, which brought consolation and strength to St. Paul, will be with us in every circumstance.

Petition Leader: Our response today is, **"Lord, give us your love and grace."**

We ask God to sustain the church when in the weakness of faith and wisdom believers dismiss the prophetic word of life. Relying on your tender mercy we pray:

We call on God's power to break through hateful attitudes that diminish the spiritual vitality of families and faith communities. Relying on your tender mercy we pray:

We implore God to renew the moral integrity of societies weakened by disregard for human life and the well-being of the poor. Relying on your tender mercy we pray:

We intercede on behalf of persons who are rendered psychologically powerless by violence and addictions. Relying on your tender mercy we pray:

We look to God's love to uphold the faith of the terminally ill that they may not despair nor succumb to suicide. Relying on your tender mercy we pray:

We entrust to God's care marriages that have weakened through emotional neglect, infidelity, and spouse abuse. Relying on your tender mercy we pray:

Presider: Gracious God, by the power of the Word and Spirit open our hearts and minds to recognize your transforming love blessing us and calling us to new life. We pray in Jesus' name.

Fourteenth Sunday in Ordinary Time (C)

Presider: Let us pray in the Spirit of Christ.

Petition Leader: Our prayer response is: **"God, our Joy, hear our prayer."**

That the rich cultural diversity of the church will be a source of spiritual nourishment and delight, we pray:

That as we travel in our own land or abroad, we will bring a blessing and be open to receiving one, we pray:

That through the word of God all nations might be made anew in unity and peace, we pray:

That the Christian community will be a healing presence in every locale, we pray:

That our boasting of Christ's love will encourage others to be nourished on the sacraments of life, we pray:

That Catholic adults will respond to the richness of our times for being of service to God's people through ordained ministries, religious life, and lay associations, we pray:

That beauty and truth will flourish in our culture through the artistic gifts and talents with which humanity has been endowed, we pray:

Presider: God, Source of our joy, receive our prayers, and through your Word nourish your life within us. We ask this in Jesus' name.

Fifteenth Sunday in Ordinary Time (A)

Presider: Let us take up in our prayers the groaning of creation that calls out for God's redeeming love.

Petition Leader: Our prayer response today is, **"Freeing God, hear us."**

We pray that the power of God's word will yield a rich harvest of holiness in the life of the church. In hope we call on God's mercy:

We ask that God's grace sustain all who proclaim the beauty and truth of God's word through the arts. In hope we call on God's mercy:

We join our voices with those who are subjected to destitution and illness through hunger and lack of quality health care. In hope we call on God's mercy:

We pray that God's transforming love will renew the health of any subjected to debilitating addictions. In hope we call on God's mercy:

We rely on God's goodness to guard our youth from all that may harm them in body and spirit. In hope we call on God's mercy:

We call upon the Holy Spirit to release nations from slavery to materialism and free them to seek the treasures of heaven. In hope we call on God's mercy:

Presider: Creating God, the beauty of your word has given us life and promises us eternity. Graciously hear our prayers, and through your Word bring us to life in the kingdom where Jesus is Lord, forever and ever.

Fifteenth Sunday in Ordinary Time (B)

Presider: Let us pray that all peoples will be filled with spiritual blessings which lead to praise of God's glorious grace.

Petition Leader: Our response today is, **"May your favor rest on us!"**

Let us pray for the blessing of a strong faith and a joyful spirit that all peoples may be loud in God's praise. Rejoicing in God's goodness, we ask:

Let us pray for the blessing of creativity that through artistic talents and gifts peoples' hearts and minds may be raised to God. Rejoicing in God's goodness, we ask:

Let us pray for the blessing of good health and happiness that our days may be lived in the fullness of physical and emotional vitality. Rejoicing in God's goodness, we ask:

Let us pray for the blessing of secure employment that heads of household may be free of financial worries for themselves and their dependents. Rejoicing in God's goodness, we ask:

Let us pray for the blessing of vocation to the ordained ministries, religious life, or lay apostolates that the gospel's joy and consolation may reach all peoples. Rejoicing in God's goodness, we ask:

Let us pray for the blessing of a compassionate heart that we may respond to the cries of the poor and address the causes of human suffering. Rejoicing in God's goodness, we ask:

Let us pray for the blessing of personal safety for our children and the elderly, for all travelers, and for any who work under hazardous conditions. Rejoicing in God's goodness, we ask:

Presider: Kind and loving God, help us to recognize your many blessings. Enable us to use your gifts to bring others to a recognition of their own blessedness. We pray in the name of the Blessed One, Jesus Christ.

Fifteenth Sunday in Ordinary Time (C)

Presider: Our personal love for God calls us to act with compassion. Let us ask God for the grace to love our neighbor as ourselves.

Petition Leader: Our response is, **"Compassionate God, give us your grace."**

That our church leaders will be guided by the Spirit as they address the causes of human suffering, we pray:

That all who have been robbed of their rights and dignity will find advocates and caregivers among the Christian faithful, we pray:

That our national and state leaders will use their influence to secure health care and social services that effectively benefit persons most in need, we pray:

That the works of mercy undertaken by religious communities and lay apostolates will attract fresh vocations, we pray:

That the Spirit will help us overcome indifference to the pressing needs of others, whether in our own country or in economically poorer nations, we pray:

That we may be generous in helping others rebuild their lives and homes after fires and natural disasters, we pray:

That the faithful departed will find consolation in the bosom of Abraham, where Lazarus is no longer poor (especially _____), we pray:

Presider: God, your gospel of compassion calls us to put into action our love for you and our neighbor. Hear our prayers, and by your Spirit make your church effective as a servant of the poor, sick, and needy of our time. We ask this in the name of Jesus, the Christ.

Sixteenth Sunday in Ordinary Time (A)

Presider: God has given us the Spirit as our helper and intercessor. In the power of the Spirit let us pray to live the gospel of salvation.

Petition Leader: Our prayer response is, **"Christ, Word of God, hear our prayer."**

Through the gospel of Jesus Christ the good seed of God's reign has been sown among us. May the world receive the gospel in faith. We pray:

Through the Holy Spirit we are led into the fullness of truth. May all who desire to know God's forgiving love be led to Christ. We pray:

Through the gospel of reconciliation the world is promised everlasting joy. May the Word inspire enemies to pursue the path to lasting peace. We pray:

Through the proclamation of the gospel the faith of the church is nurtured. May the eucharist strengthen our discipleship with Christ. We pray:

Through the Word-Made-Flesh the kindness of God has appeared among us. May our acts of kindness continue to reveal God's justice. We pray:

Through the resurrection of Jesus the mercy of God is fully revealed. May all the dead rise at God's word to the glory of heaven. We pray:

Presider: Redeeming God, you have given us your Word and Spirit to lead us to you. Receive our prayers, for we desire to share your life completely in the reign of heaven. We ask this in Jesus' name.

Sixteenth Sunday in Ordinary Time (B)

Presider: We are called to live a new humanity in the Spirit of Jesus. Let us pray to be faithful witnesses to this good news.

Petition Leader: Our prayer response today will be a moment of silent intercession. [Leader, please allow for a sufficient pause after each petition.]

Let us pray for a courageous faith that we may exercise justice and care in all our affairs.

Let us pray for an deepening of hope in the triumph of goodness when we experience hatred and ill will in others.

Let us pray to be more loving that we may continue to dismantle social barriers erected by racism, sexism, and selfishness.

Let us pray for an increase of self-respect that leads to physically, spiritually, and morally healthy relationships and lifestyles.

Let us pray for all religious leaders and those entrusted with pastoral care of God's people that their ministry may witness to Christ's compassion.

Let us pray for the wisdom to recognize when our bodies and minds require rest and to claim quiet spaces for personal renewal.

Let us embrace in prayer the sick, those who are dying, and all who have passed from this life.

Presider: Loving God, your good news revives us in spirit. May we cling to the new life your love offers and nourish it with constant prayer in Jesus' name.

Sixteenth Sunday in Ordinary Time (C)

Presider: The mystery of Christ in us moves us to pray for the church.

Petition Leader: Our response is, **"Abba God, hear our prayer ."**

May the Spirit of Wisdom guide Pope *[name]* and the bishops of the church in their apostolic ministry of building up the body of Christ. We pray:

May the Holy Spirit give us a love for the word of God that we will be, like Mary of Bethany, faithful disciples of the compassionate Christ. We pray:

May the grace of God help us to cultivate a personal relationship with Christ as we, like Martha of Bethany, carry out lives of loving service to others. We pray:

May the consoling Spirit draw Christians into deeper union with Christ through any personal sufferings in body, mind, or spirit. We pray:

May the empowering Spirit enable all ministers of the gospel to proclaim the word of God's peace and compassion in its fullness. We pray:

May the Spirit of loving kindness move the Christian community to offer hospitality to strangers, especially the immigrant in our midst. We pray:

Presider: God, whose Spirit is Truth, hear our prayers. May the mystery of Christ in us flourish to your honor and glory. We pray through Jesus Christ, our Redeemer.

Seventeenth Sunday in Ordinary Time (A)

Presider: God invited Solomon to ask for something. Christ, also, taught that we should ask if we want to receive. Let us pray for gifts in keeping with God's riches.

Petition Leader: Our prayer response is, **"God, hear our prayer."**

For the gift of a courageous faith that the church will constantly strive to fulfill God's will in all things. We pray:

For the gift of hope that all who seek the reign of God will not be discouraged in time of doubt and spiritual darkness. We pray:

For the gift of love for God that we may be spiritually alive in Christ, the first-born of many sisters and brothers. We pray:

For the gift of wisdom that all who serve in public office may perform their duties with understanding and moral integrity. We pray:

For the gift of reverence that all godly people may display respect for God's word and creation and especially the dignity of others. We pray:

For the gift of knowledge that young and old may discern what is good and holy before God. We pray:

For the gift of compassion that our hearts may respond to the cries of all who suffer. We pray:

Presider: God of goodness and love, may we cherish the gifts you give us to draw us to yourself. By the power of your Spirit keep us alive in Christ and persevering in prayer. Grant this in the name of Jesus, our mediator with you.

Seventeenth Sunday in Ordinary Time (B)

Presider: Let us take to heart the apostle's teachings and pray for a deepening of love as God's people.

Petition Leader: Our prayer response today is, **"Christ, hear our prayer."**

Christ has established one body of believers to sing God's praises. May the body of Christ throughout the world grow in unity and love. We pray:

God has lavished one Spirit upon the world. May we rejoice in the diversity of gifts that flow from the Spirit's creativity. We pray:

All humanity is called to one hope. May nations set their hearts on the blessings of the reign of heaven. We pray:

God has given the world one Savior. May Christ who was raised up for us draw all peoples into the redeeming love of God. We pray:

We are called to walk in the light of one faith. May this gift inspire us to place our gifts in service of others. We pray:

Through one baptism we have become a new creation. May our rebirth in Christ be our inspiration for creating inclusive communities of compassion. We pray:

One God and Creator has given us life. May we uphold human dignity and reverence each person out of love for God. We pray:

Presider: God, our Creator and Redeemer, hear our prayers, and through the Spirit of unity regenerate all lives in the peace of Jesus Christ, who lives and reigns with you and the Holy Spirit, one God forever and ever.

Seventeenth Sunday in Ordinary Time (C)

Presider: God lavishes the Spirit upon those who ask. Let us pray that the Spirit will be given abundantly to the church and the world.

Petition Leader: Our prayer response is: **"God, may your grace abound in us."**

As the church nourishes its faith in your saving power through the daily bread of your word, we pray:

As the church carries on Christ's ministry of reconciliation to those alienated from your peace, we pray:

As the church ministers through prayer and sacrament to those who are sick and suffering, we pray:

As world leaders strive to deter terrorism and violence, we pray:

As societies struggle to address the needs of the economically poor, we pray:

As cities work to promote the safety of their citizens, we pray:

As we use these summer months for vacation and rest, we pray:

Presider: God, may your Spirit abound in us that we may persevere in prayer. Receive our prayers through Christ, who has restored us to life in you.

Eighteenth Sunday in Ordinary Time (A)

Presider: In Christ, God has renewed the promises made to David. As a people of the covenant in Christ's blood let us intercede for the church and the world.

Petition Leader: Today's prayer response is: **"Uphold us in your love, O God."**

Through Catholic health care systems and the church's healing ministries may those who suffer experience God's tender mercies. We ask in faith:

Through the collaborative work of church and civic leaders may religious and political persecution diminish throughout the world. We ask in faith:

Through our generosity may the efforts of humanitarian organizations to reduce hunger at home and abroad continue. We ask in faith:

Through the grace of God may our personal trials be moments to deepen our prayerful reliance on God's care. We ask in faith:

Through our celebration of the eucharist may our thirst for communion with God and neighbor be satisfied. We ask in faith:

Through the dying and rising of Jesus may all the dead come to the unity and peace of God's kingdom (especially _____). We ask in faith:

Presider: Merciful God, so great is your love for us that nothing can come between us except sin. Accept our prayers. Help us to remain strong in faith, hope, and love that we may delight in the rich fare of the heavenly banquet. We ask this in the name of Jesus, our Savior.

Eighteenth Sunday in Ordinary Time (B)

Presider: Let us pray that the world will be spiritually renewed through the power of God's Word and Spirit.

Petition Leader: Our prayer response today is, **"Christ, Bread of God, hear us!"**

For all who work to create new bonds of love and respect among peoples; may societies cast aside the old ways of superiority and discrimination. In faith we call out:

For all whose human labors are invested in the perishable things of this passing life; may the word of God inspire peoples to invest themselves in God's work. In faith we call out:

For all who hunger for spiritual vitality; may the bread of God's word and the life of the Spirit lead them to deeper intimacy with Christ. In faith we call out:

For persons who struggle to remain sober and drug-free; may the strengthening Spirit uphold them in good health. In faith we call out:

For all who have experienced a spiritual rebirth and are eager to live anew their baptismal faith; may their enthusiasm find welcome among us. In faith we call out:

For those who appear before Christ hungry for eternal life; may the One who is sealed by the resurrection welcome the dead into heaven's banquet (particularly _____). In faith we call out:

Presider: God, receive our prayers through Jesus Christ, your chosen servant whose words nourish our faith, hope, and love.

Eighteenth Sunday in Ordinary Time (C)

Presider: Let us pray for the spiritual gifts that enable us to grow rich in God's sight.

Petition Leader: Our prayer response is: **"Giver of gifts, hear our prayer."**

For the gift of love that re-creates us to be an inclusive community in Christ. We ask in faith:

For the gift of honesty that frees us to speak the truth in love. We ask in faith:

For the gift of respect that will help us honor each person's dignity and life. We ask in faith:

For the gift of moderation that we may use wisely the earth's resources. We ask in faith:

For the gift of generosity that raises us above greed and selfish pursuits. We ask in faith:

For the gift of chastity that we may live reverently in a sexually permissive culture. We ask in faith:

For the gift of eternal life that all the dead, whose lives were hidden in Christ, may rejoice in glory. We ask in faith:

Presider: God in heaven, your Word and Spirit bring us the gift of your life. Receive our prayers and fill us with the gifts that draw us to you. We pray in Jesus' name.

Nineteenth Sunday in Ordinary Time (A)

Presider: Let us pray that true faith will flourish everywhere.

Petition Leader: Our response today is, **"Christ Jesus, save us."**

In time of trial and turmoil we ask God to strengthen Pope *[name]* that he may give encouraging witness to his brother bishops and all the faithful. Like Peter we call out:

In periods of insecurity and uncertainty we ask God to sustain the church's hope in Christ's redeeming love. Like Peter we call out:

In the darkest hours of our spiritual journey to the farther shore, we ask that the Spirit of Jesus bring us interior peace. Like Peter we call out:

In our encounters with forces that threaten human life we ask God for the courage to take risks for world peace and nonviolent living. Like Peter we call out:

In our struggle to overcome debilitating fears we ask God to speak gently to our hearts in prayer. Like Peter we call out:

In moments when we have experienced the calming love of Jesus in the Spirit, may we not withhold our public praise for salvation. Like Peter we call out:

Presider: God of heaven and earth, hear your people's prayer to be sustained by the saving presence of Christ. We ask this in the name of the One who invites our trust, Jesus Christ, the Son of God.

Nineteenth Sunday in Ordinary Time (B)

Presider: Let us pray to pursue the way of love that the church and world will more perfectly image Christ.

Petition Leader: Our response today is, **"Jesus, Living Bread, renew us."**

When discouragement plagues human life and death seems more appealing, may we not settle down in despair. We intercede with Christ and ask:

When hostilities and dissension wreck havoc with the stability of our faith communities, may the Spirit's peace flourish anew. We intercede with Christ and ask:

When the teachings of the gospel challenge our thinking and invite us to deeper conversion, may God's word be our light. We intercede with Christ and ask:

When our spiritual resources seem insufficient for the journey in faith, may we recognize the sustenance God sends our way. We intercede with Christ and ask:

When tenderness, kindness, and forgiveness are overpowered by bitterness, anger, and revenge, may the healing Spirit move upon our minds and hearts. We intercede with Christ and ask:

When we are at the end of our earthly journey, may Jesus, who gave his life for the world, bid us welcome into the heavenly feast. We intercede with Christ and ask:

Presider: Christ Jesus, may your Spirit uphold us through the many seasons of life. Renew in us the joy of your love that with you we may be a pleasing gift to God. You live and reign forever and ever.

Nineteenth Sunday in Ordinary Time (C)

Presider: Confident that our faith finds favor with God we raise our voices and call on God's kindness.

Petition Leader: Our response will be a moment of silent prayer following each petition. [Leader, please allow for a sufficient pause after each petition.]

For a deepening of trust in the promptings of the Spirit who gives life to our journey in faith.

For an increase in hope that sustains us through periods of unknowing and uncertainty.

For a revitalizing of the spiritual life in those who have lost sight of God's reign.

For diligence that keeps us open and attentive to God's presence breaking into our lives.

For blessings upon all who serve our communities in emergency medical units.

For the gift of preparedness should death come without warning.

For the personal needs and concerns that we carry in our hearts today.

Presider: God, in faith we await the salvation of the just. We offer our prayers in the sure and certain hope of arriving at the heavenly city where Jesus is Lord, forever and ever.

Twentieth Sunday in Ordinary Time (A)

Presider: Let us join in the priestly prayer of Jesus that all may be one in the household of faith.

Petition Leader: Our prayer response today is, **"Savior of all, hear us!"**

For the church as it undertakes Christ's ministry of reconciliation; may we use our spiritual gifts to create inclusive communities of love and care. We pray:

For greater rejoicing in God's unlimited mercy; may the conversion of others unite us in common praise of God's holy name. We pray:

For those ordained for service to the church; may the ministry of bishops, priests, and deacons foster greater unity among God's people. We pray:

For non-Christians who seek God's healing love through the church's works of mercy; may race or creed not hinder Christians from responding with compassion to the cries of the poor. We pray:

For all of us who hold fast to the covenant of love in the blood of Christ; may our celebration of eucharist strengthen our resolve to act with justice. We pray:

For parents who invoke God's power to restore the spiritual and physical well-being of their children; may God receive their prayer of faith. We pray:

Presider: Loving God, in faith we call out for your saving power so beautifully revealed in Christ. May our prayers be pleasing in your sight and be received in the name of the Savior, Jesus Christ.

Twentieth Sunday in Ordinary Time (B)

Presider: Let us pray for Wisdom's guidance and insight that lead to spiritual maturity.

Petition Leader: Our prayer response today is, **"God, guide us by your Spirit."**

Bless Pope *[name]* and all bishops with the gifts of knowledge that their teaching ministry will build up the church in truth and justice. Trusting in your goodness, we ask:

Guide the work of theologians that their vision and insights may serve the spiritual growth of the Christian community. Trusting in your goodness, we ask:

Bestow the Spirit's counsel upon the Archdiocese/Diocese of _____ that our local church may be a leaven for justice and spiritually rich in love for God and neighbor. Trusting in your goodness, we ask:

Enlighten by the Spirit's grace public officials and all whose decisions affect social life that they may serve the common good with wisdom and truth. Trusting in your goodness, we ask:

Enrich the intellectual and spiritual gifts of all educators that they may be instruments of human goodness. Trusting in your goodness, we ask:

Draw to the table of your love the peoples of the world that all lives may be nourished on the living bread of Christ. Trusting in your goodness, we ask:

Seat at the heavenly banquet all who desired to feast on your eternal mercies (especially _____). Trusting in your goodness, we ask:

Presider: Nurturing God, to you we owe our hymns of praise and thanksgiving, for you have called us to feast at Wisdom's table. Hear our prayers and guide all creation by your Spirit. Grant this through Jesus, our Bread of Life.

Twentieth Sunday in Ordinary Time (C)

Presider: Let us pray that the Christ-kindled fires of faith, hope, and love will renew the face of the earth.

Petition Leader: Our prayer response is, **"God, hear us."**

For the church's leaders as they attend to the emerging spiritual needs of all members; may the Spirit of the Second Vatican Council guide their ministry. We pray:

For the community of believers in the resurrection; may opposition to the gospel not deter the church from serving all peoples. We pray:

For those who struggle to be free from addictions; may the healing love of Christ be their sustenance. We pray:

For troubled marriages; may God's wisdom guide husbands and wives as they address conflicts and problems. We pray:

For families and communities divided over religious issues; may the Spirit of unity lead us to God's peace. We pray:

For parents who have abandoned their children emotionally, morally, or physically; may human weakness be overcome through renewed faith in God's transforming grace. We pray:

Presider: God, your Word came to enliven in us the fire of your love. Hear our prayers and strengthen your church to walk in the light of one faith and one Spirit. We ask this in the name of Jesus, your servant and our Savior.

Twenty-First Sunday in Ordinary Time (A)

Presider: Jesus affirmed the bedrock of Peter's faith. Let us pray that our faith in Christ will build up the church in love.

Petition Leader: Our prayer response today is, **"Christ Jesus, hear our prayer!"**

Jesus, like Peter, the church professes that you are the Messiah. May our words become actions that bring your life to the world. We pray:

In Peter you have given your household a sure servant. May the apostolic ministry of Pope *[name]*, servant of the servants of God, uphold your church in peace and unity. We pray:

Like Peter, the teachers of the church profess you are the Christ. Sustain bishops and theologians by the Spirit's wisdom as they apply the truths of faith to issues of our time. We pray:

Like Peter, your disciples profess you are God's Anointed. Confirm in the church's vowed religious and clergy gifts in keeping with the riches of God's glory. We pray:

Like Peter, the faithful acknowledge that you are the Son of the living God. May our celebration of the eucharist express our gratitude for your love. We pray:

Like Peter, our faith can falter in time of trial. Renew in grace any whose trust in your love has begun to falter. We pray:

Presider: Saving God, receive our prayers that we make in the name of your beloved, Jesus the Messiah, who lives and reigns forever and ever.

Twenty-First Sunday in Ordinary Time (B)

Presider: Believing that Christ has the words that lead to fullness of life, let us pray to be faithful to the gospel we have heard.

Petition Leader: Our response today is, **"Living Word, hear our prayer."**

We believe your Word gives life; may the church proclaim the gospel of life in the power of your Spirit. In faith we pray:

We believe your Word nourishes human hopes; may peoples whose lives are plagued by oppression and pain find healing in the good news. In faith we pray:

We believe your Word reconciles all humanity into the peace of God's reign; may all nations walk by the light of truth. In faith we pray:

We believe your Word is Spirit and life; may we who feast of your sacramental presence experience the power of your transforming love. In faith we pray:

We believe that your Word creates us anew; may all our relationships, especially Christian marriages, be shaped by your example of self-giving love. In faith we pray:

We believe that at your Word the faithful will rise to the glory of the resurrection; may our sisters and brothers who have died be welcomed into the new creation (especially_____). In faith we pray:

Presider: God our Creator, you have birthed us through your word and redeemed us through Christ, the Word of Life. Hear our prayers, increase our faith, and by the Spirit lead us to all truth. Grant this through Christ, our Lord.

Twenty-First Sunday in Ordinary Time (C)

Presider: Let us pray that the word of God we hear today will help us in our daily living.

Petition Leader: Our prayer response is, **"Help us to live your word, Lord."**

May love for God's word bring diverse peoples together in a unified household of faith. Trusting in your mercy, we ask:

May all Christians be open to the challenge of the gospel and fashion lifestyles according to its commands. Trusting in your mercy, we ask:

May parents, Catholic educators, and catechists create for youth pathways that lead to morally and spiritually healthy lives. Trusting in your mercy, we ask:

May adults who physically and psychologically abuse children as a form of discipline follow the way of Christ, who taught compassion. Trusting in your mercy, we ask:

May young people who are at risk of addictive and self-destructive behaviors find in the Christian community a strengthening peace. Trusting in your mercy, we ask:

May all who eat and drink at the table of the eucharist live its mystery in their daily lives. Trusting in your mercy, we ask:

Presider: God of all creation, your word calls us to life in the reign of heaven. Through your grace may we live its truth and come to the peace it offers on earth and in heaven. We pray in the name of Christ, your Word-Among-Us, who lives and reigns forever and ever.

Twenty-Second Sunday in Ordinary Time (A)

Presider: Let us ask for the grace of God that we may be transformed by the Word of Life.

Petition Leader: Our response today is, **"God of our journey, be with us."**

For the church that is called to be one with the sacrifice of Christ; may our spiritual worship strengthen us for discipleship. We pray:

For the gift of desire for union with God; may we know a holy restlessness that moves our hearts to seek the Lord. We pray:

For increased harmony among all peoples; may these years (leading to/of) the new millennium be a time of universal spiritual renewal. We pray:

For those who attempt to gain the world through power and self-promotion; may the cross of Christ reveal the way to lasting treasures in the reign of heaven. We pray:

For students young and old; may each be given the gifts and talents needed to grow as whole persons in body, mind, and spirit. We pray:

For the tenacity to proclaim God's word of peace; may the Spirit give to all Christian teachers the courage to call the world back to God as did the prophets of old. We pray:

Presider: God, our Creator, be with us on our life's journey. As Christ, your Beloved, took the path to Jerusalem, so may we follow the paths that lead to eternal life. Grant our prayer in Jesus' name.

Twenty-Second Sunday in Ordinary Time (B)

Presider: Let us pray to have the heart and mind of Christ.

Petition Leader: Our prayer response today is, **"God of light, hear us."**

For the community of believers in the gospel of salvation; may the church act on the law of love as Christ commanded. We pray:

For a deeper reverence and knowledge of the sacred scriptures, that God's word will guide us in discerning the essentials of love. We pray:

For the ability to set aside human traditions and religious customs out of deference to the gospel's call to justice and compassion. We pray:

For the gift of spiritual and moral renewal in our personal lives, that all our actions may flow from God's peace and truth. We pray:

For all who are college-bound, that the Spirit will guide their lives and continue claiming them for Christ. We pray:

For all of us as we gather at this table of life, that our worship of God may be rooted in sincerity of heart. We pray:

Presider: God of glory, purify us by your Word that our lives may be holy, our actions just, and our prayers acceptable. Through Christ, our Lord.

Twenty-Second Sunday in Ordinary Time (C)

Presider: Christ is our covenant of peace. With confidence let us call upon the Lord who shows us the way to the reign of God.

Petition Leader: Our prayer response is, **"Christ Jesus, guide us."**

Savior of all, we draw near to you in this meal. By your Word and Spirit light our way to even greater intimacy with all that is holy. With trust we ask:

Light to the nations, you taught that the greater among us should be as the servant. May wealthier nations help build up countries struggling to rise from oppression and poverty. With trust we ask:

Word of Life, your gospel leads to the city of the living God. Enable political and religious leaders to follow your way. With trust we ask:

Life-giving Word, help us to walk humbly with God and avoid presumption in our social and religious behaviors. With trust we ask:

Compassion of God, you call us to freely share our blessings with persons who have less. May your generous hospitality remain alive in us. With trust we ask:

Servant of God's mercy, you came to raise up a fallen world. Bring our beloved dead into the festal gathering of heaven (especially _____). With trust we ask:

Presider: Christ, you are a home for the sinner and the forsaken. May we, who are your disciples, open our hearts and homes to others and be worthy of welcome in the heavenly Jerusalem, where you live and reign forever and ever.

Twenty-Third Sunday in Ordinary Time (A)

Presider: Assured by the gospel that Christ is in the midst of the community at prayer, we raise our voices in intercession.

Petition Leader: Our response is, **"Christ, our Justice, hear us."**

For the church as it discerns the moral implication of scientific and medical technology; may it teach with wisdom and grace. We pray:

For the courage to warn the sinner; may we not cower from challenging that which we know is wrong. We pray:

For the spiritual maturity to recognize the universal dimensions of loving our neighbor, especially nations that are plagued by poverty. We pray:

For moral integrity in marriages; may spouses hold fast to their promise to honor and respect each other. We pray:

For an increase of respect for others' property rights; may we continue to instruct our youth that shoplifting, vandalism, and plagiarism are acts of injustice. We pray:

For Christians in corporate business and other professions; may they witness to the highest ethical principles in large and small matters. We pray:

Presider: Just God, you call all people to pursue justice and to love one another. Receive our prayers and guide us as we walk humbly in your presence. Grant this through Christ, our Savior.

Twenty-Third Sunday in Ordinary Time (B)

Presider: Gathered as the body of Christ, let our prayers embrace the church and the world.

Petition Leader: Our prayer response today is, **"Redeeming God, be our light."**

By your Spirit endow Pope *[name]*, all bishops, and pastors with the wisdom to guide believers to greater unity and peace. We ask in faith:

By your Word enable all Christians to rise above alienating attitudes that diminish the bonds of friendship and care to which we are called. We ask in faith:

By the power of your love working through all people of goodwill, help our world to flourish spiritually. We ask in faith:

By your healing love open the ear of the human heart to hear the cries of the poor. We ask in faith:

By the light of your truth help us to safeguard the earth and to foster lifestyles that respect our natural resources. We ask in faith:

By the power of Christ's resurrection bring all the dead to the joy of eternal life (especially _____). We ask in faith:

Presider: Indwelling God, your presence calls us to be holy and compassionate. Help us to live the mystery of Christ in whose name we pray, now and forever.

Twenty-Third Sunday in Ordinary Time (C)

Presider: Let us call upon God to lavish the Spirit of wisdom upon our church and world.

Petition Leader: Our invocation is, **"God, send us your Spirit of wisdom."**

God, uphold all who work as international negotiators for peace and reconciliation among enemies. We pray:

Strengthen Pope *[name]* and bishops of the church as they appeal for the life of those condemned to death. We pray:

Enlighten with good counsel those who seek to discern your will, particularly those contemplating marriage or religious vocations. We pray:

Lovingly nurture the life of faith served through the church's prison ministry. We pray:

Comfort us when our commitment to Christ alienates us from people we love. We pray:

Enable Christians to affirm all people begotten in Christ as brothers and sisters without distinction to race or social standing. We pray:

Presider: God of love, through your Holy Spirit draw us into deeper intimacy with Christ that we may live your word in its fullness. Grant our prayers through Christ, our Lord.

Twenty-Fourth Sunday in Ordinary Time (A)

Presider: The gospel calls us to compassionate living. Let us pray for the grace to be rich in mercy.

Petition Leader: Our prayer response is, **"Christ, may we be merciful."**

We are called by the gospel to live responsibly. May we use our spiritual strengths to foster lifestyles that conform to the law of Christ. We ask in faith:

We entrust to God's care Pope *[name]* and the bishops of the world as they mediate peace between enemies. May their ministry extend Christ's work of reconciliation. We ask in faith:

We pray for the grace to let go of hurts that keep wounds from healing. May the Spirit of Christ set us free from clinging to animosity. We ask in faith:

We ask blessing for therapists and psychologists dedicated to helping victims of violence. May they be instruments of the consoling work of the Spirit. We ask in faith:

We pray for all who participate in organized crime and violent retaliation. May the power of God bring about a complete change of heart. We ask in faith:

We implore God's saving love to intervene in the lives of persons and groups entangled in drugs and prostitution. May the Spirit's power guide them to new life in Christ. We ask in faith:

Presider: Gracious God, hear our prayers for the gift of mercy. May your compassion accompany us through life and death. We ask this in the name of Jesus, in whom we have plentiful redemption.

Twenty-Fourth Sunday in Ordinary Time (B)

Presider: Our profession of faith calls us to share in Christ's mission of salvation for the life of the world. Let us entrust our calling to God's care.

Petition Leader: Our response today is, **"Lord, uphold your servants."**

May the gift of faith enliven the church's commitment to justice on behalf of the economically poor of the world. Trusting that God is with us, we ask:

May church organizations and ministries dedicated to the works of mercy find plentiful support from God's people. Trusting that God works through us, we ask:

May the Spirit sustain the church when our faith meets with resentment, hostility, or ridicule. Trusting that God accompanies us, we ask:

May Christians in government and roles of public service be forerunners in fostering public policies that serve the most needy. Trusting that God depends on us, we ask:

May the grace of God be our strength when we are tempted to avoid our personal share in the hardships of living gospel truths. Trusting that God helps us in our weakness, we ask:

May our care and support for persons and communities rebuilding their lives from tragedies and disasters be a channel of God's consoling love. Trusting that God heals us, we ask:

Presider: God, we depend on your love and grace for all things. Receive our prayers that our faith may be life-giving to others. We pray in Jesus' name.

Twenty-Fourth Sunday in Ordinary Time (C)

Presider: Let us implore God to grant overflowing grace to all people.

Petition Leader: Our prayer response is, **"God, hear our prayer for mercy."**

We implore God to give the grace of conversion to any who value the passing things of earth more highly than the everlasting life of heaven. We pray:

May God help us overcome any spiritual arrogance that impedes true unity among us. We pray:

May God's love win back the hearts of young people who have wandered far from the life of grace and peace. We pray:

May our experience of God's mercy enable us to be more merciful to others. We pray:

May we not hold people's past deeds against them when they have returned to Christ and the sacraments of the church. We pray:

May the dead come to life in the reign of heaven (especially_____). We pray:

Presider: Compassionate God, hear our prayer for your mercy. Enable our lives to be rooted in your saving will. We ask this in the name of Jesus Christ, our Peacemaker with you.

Twenty-Fifth Sunday in Ordinary Time (A)

Presider: Let us call on the Holy Spirit to help us live in accord with the gospel.

Petition Leader: Our response today will be a moment of silent prayer. [Leader, please allow for a sufficient pause after each petition.]

Let us ask for the grace to recognize our spiritual gifts and to use them wisely.

Let us pray for the spiritual strength to accept God's gracious will that we may heal from our losses and rise from our grief.

Let us ask that God's grace be with all who are searching for lasting truths.

Let us remember persons struggling to rise from self-destructive behaviors, particularly all who are in periods of recovery from addictions.

Let us uphold in prayer the seriously ill, especially newborns and children, their families, doctors, and nurses.

Let us pray to be free from envy and jealousy and to rejoice in God's love.

Let us remember those who have died, particularly those who leave this world without immediate family or friends.

Presider: God, your ways are life-giving. Receive our prayers and sustain us by your Spirit of love. We ask this in Jesus' name.

Twenty-Fifth Sunday in Ordinary Time (B)

Presider: Let us pray.

Petition Leader: Our prayer response today is, **"Christ, our Justice, have mercy."**

For Christian communities; may our churches be free of hatred, which deadens the spirit. We pray:

For healing from all jealousy and greed; may these deadly viruses of the spiritual life not be found among the disciples of Jesus. We pray:

For missionaries who are tortured and put to death because of their commitment to justice; may the witness of contemporary martyrs spur us onward. We pray:

For persons who would use religion and church positions for personal gain; may the example of Christ transform all self-seeking into self-giving. We pray:

For wisdom and sincerity in our personal prayer life; may the Spirit teach us how to seek the spiritual gifts that serve God's will and the common good. We pray:

For the sick and the economically poor who live in radical dependence on God's care; may their trust be an inspiration to our faith. We pray:

Presider: Christ Jesus, you are the Just One, who calls us to be a servant church. Show us your mercy and love that we may live in accord with your Spirit, for you live and reign forever and ever.

Twenty-Fifth Sunday in Ordinary Time (C)

Presider: Let us pray, as the apostle instructed, particularly imploring God to make us instruments of peace.

Petition Leader: Our response is, **"God, give us your love for justice."**

Christ has entrusted his saving mission to the church. May all the baptized strive to introduce God's freeing love into every human relationship. We pray:

Christ has revealed that God's justice lifts up the poor. May we use our influence to safeguard unskilled laborers from exploitation in the workplace. We pray:

Discipleship with Christ has no boundaries. May Christians in corporate business, technology, and political positions serve the common good. We pray:

The gospel calls us to be peacemakers. May our elected leaders search out the causes of social unrest and work to restore tranquillity to all citizens. We pray:

Christ promises us lasting wealth in the reign of heaven. May we use wisely the blessings God gives us on our pilgrimage. We pray:

God's word invites us to pray in thanksgiving for every human life. May our prayer express itself in actions that uphold human life and keep sacred the memory of the dead. We pray:

Presider: God of heaven and earth, help us to live free from anger and dissension in our private and public lives. Receive our prayers and keep us faithful to Christ's mission of mercy. We pray in the name of Jesus.

Twenty-Sixth Sunday in Ordinary Time (A)

Presider: Let us pray for a deepening of love, unity, and peace in our lives.

Petition Leader: Our prayer response is, **"Loving God, hear our prayer."**

That our mutual love for one another will deepen our bonds of spiritual communion in the blood of Christ, we pray:

That the grace of conversion will renew nations in God's peace, we pray:

That racial and gender superiority will be replaced with genuine respect for diversity, we pray:

That families will be centers of harmony rather than rivalry and resentment, we pray:

That self-centered wants will mature into personal commitments to seek the common good, we pray:

That the support extended to the terminally ill by loving and compassionate caregivers will be a sign of God's own care, we pray:

Presider: Saving God, by your Spirit of love and peace, help us to have the heart and mind of Christ. Grant this through Christ, our Redeemer.

Twenty-Sixth Sunday in Ordinary Time (B)

Presider: Only by the power of God's Spirit can we lead holy, prophetic, and compassionate lives. Let us implore the Spirit to be with us on our journey.

Petition Leader: After each petition let us invoke the Paraclete, saying, **"Spirit of Jesus, be with us."**

As the church labors to expel the demons of violence and poverty that destroy human life, we ask:

As Christian communions work to deepen the spiritual and sacramental bonds among all the followers of Christ, we ask:

As we take to heart the word of God calling us away from extravagant living and all forms of wastefulness, we ask:

As we struggle with our own constant need for conversion that leads to fullness of life in the reign of God, we ask:

As societies labor to build healthier environments, especially for infants and children, we ask:

As we pray to be renewed in the love of Christ celebrated in this sacred meal, we ask:

As we return our beloved dead to the earth in the sure and certain hope of resurrection (especially_____), we ask:

Presider: Gracious God, may your Spirit dwell in our hearts through faith that we may be one with Christ in his mission of mercy. We ask you to receive our prayers in Jesus' name.

Twenty-Sixth Sunday in Ordinary Time (C)

Presider: Christ is the Beloved of God, the One to whom we are called to listen. Let us pray to keep the love command of Christ, thereby fulfilling the law and the prophets.

Petition Leader: Our response is, **"Keep us faithful to your command, O Christ."**

We are called to be God's people striving toward eternal life. May we pursue integrity of word and deed in our lives. We pray:

The prophets denounced those who remained indifferent to the poor. May we bear witness to the compassion of Christ and not fail in our prophetic vocation. We pray:

Lazarus was covered with sores and in need of medical care. May the church continue to advocate that all of the needy receive adequate health care. We pray:

Lazarus lay at the gate of the wealthy individual. May Christian communities in every locale be prompt in securing shelter for those in need. We pray:

Lazarus longed to eat scraps from the table of plenty. May we, who feast at the eucharistic table, work diligently to assure that all persons enjoy the goods of creation. We pray:

The rich individual's lack of care led to alienation from God. May our love for our neighbor in need lead us to everlasting intimacy with Christ. We pray:

Presider: God of mercy, in you Lazarus has found unending consolation. Keep us faithful to your way of love so that the poor can present us to Christ when our life is ended. Hear our prayers in Jesus' name.

Twenty-Seventh Sunday in Ordinary Time (A)

Presider: In a spirit of gratitude let us place our petitions before God, whose love is everlasting.

Petition Leader: Our response is, **"God, in your mercy, hear us."**

We pray that our love for God's word will enable us to bring forth a rich harvest of justice. In faith we call out:

We pray that Christian communities will be vibrant centers of prayer and praise. In faith we call out:

We pray that the Spirit of God will guide world leaders as they seek ways to promote respect and peace among nations. In faith we call out:

We pray that the media and entertainment industry will reaffirm decency and nonviolence in its service to the public. In faith we call out:

We pray that debilitating anxiety will be overcome by greater trust in God's providential care. In faith we call out:

We pray that educators will cultivate in youth a desire for all that is excellent, true, beautiful, and holy. In faith we call out:

Presider: God of peace, in faith we pray and ask that the Spirit of holiness guide our lives. Grant our prayers through Christ, our Redeemer.

Twenty-Seventh Sunday in Ordinary Time (B)

Presider: Rejoicing in the one faith, one baptism, and one God who is over all of us, let us pray that all creation will live in peace and unity.

Petition Leader: In the unity of our faith let us ask, **"Saving God, hear our prayer."**

Crowned with glory and honor, Christ has full authority over the new creation. May we set our hearts on the reign of heaven where peace endures forever. We humbly ask:

Fashioned to live in mutual respect and harmony, may men and women of goodwill and integrity promote decency that eliminates racial and sexual discrimination, especially in the workplace. We humbly ask:

United in the mystery of Christ, may the mutual love of Christian spouses be a source of blessing to their families and to society. We humbly ask:

Mindful of our human weakness, may troubled marriages and all struggling to heal from divorce draw strength from the compassion of God. We humbly ask:

Inspired by the example of Jesus, may all who are called to be teachers in the faith open doors to the sacred for children and any who seek God. We humbly ask:

Raised up for our salvation, may Christ lead all our beloved dead to the glory promised to all God's people (especially _____). We humbly ask:

Presider: Merciful God, your Word created us and raised us up. Receive our prayers and sustain your pilgrim people in the Spirit of love and peace. We ask this in the name of Jesus, our Savior and brother.

Twenty-Seventh Sunday in Ordinary Time (C)

Presider: Let us pray that God's gifts will keep us strong in faith, hope, and love.

Petition Leader: Our prayer response is, **"Indwelling Spirit, help us."**

The Spirit God gives is no cowardly spirit. Let us stir into flame the gift of faith by which we give public witness to our love for God. We ask in faith:

The Spirit God gives is no indifferent spirit. Let us stir into flame the gift of compassion by which we show forth true love of neighbor. We ask out of love:

The Spirit God gives is no blind spirit. Let us stir into flame the gift of justice that enables us to envision creation healed of its misery. We ask in hope:

The Spirit God gives is no violent spirit. Let us stir into flame the gift of peace that we may walk in integrity before God. We humbly ask:

The Spirit God gives is no unholy spirit. Let us stir into flame the gift of wisdom that we may be transformed by God's word. We ask in faith:

The Spirit God gives is no destructive spirit. Let us stir into flame the gift of reverence for God's creation. We ask out of love:

The Spirit God gives is no rebellious spirit. Let us stir into flame the gift of service that God's way may be fulfilled. We ask in faith:

Presider: God, guard us with your Spirit and keep us strong in faith. Hear our prayers, for we desire to do your will with the help of your grace, through Christ, our Redeemer.

Twenty-Eighth Sunday in Ordinary Time (A)

Presider: God is our strength and salvation. Let us call upon God's love to safeguard our church and world.

Petition Leader: Our response today is, **"God, our strength, hear us."**

May the baptized, who are called to feast on the riches of Christ, be generous distributors of God's gracious love. We pray:

May persons who are brought low by poverty and illness draw strength from the sacraments of the church and its works of compassion. We pray:

May Christians be united in removing the veil of death caused by violence and injustice. We pray:

May our love for Christ move us to invite others into the household of faith. We pray:

May families that are grieving be fortified by the Spirit of compassion. We pray:

May professionals who help others cope with crisis and loss through psychological, counseling, and social services be instruments of God's care. We pray:

May the dead who have trusted in God's mercy rejoice at the wedding feast of heaven (especially _____). We pray:

Presider: Redeeming God, we look to you for every grace and blessing. Receive our prayers and uphold us in Christ, our Lord.

Twenty-Eighth Sunday in Ordinary Time (B)

Presider: Like Solomon, let us pray for Wisdom and desire her presence above earthly treasures.

Petition Leader: Our invocation today is, **"Send forth your Spirit of wisdom."**

We ask for your kindly Spirit to guide us in our daily living that our families may abide in peace and friendship. In hope we call out:

We pray for the Spirit's purity that we may safeguard human dignity from ill will and violence. In hope we call out:

We invoke the Spirit of justice that our legislative and judicial systems may serve the common good and the needs of the economically poor. In hope we call out:

We implore the Spirit of right judgment to accompany all medical and scientific researchers that they may hold to the highest ethical principles. In hope we call out:

We ask the Spirit of God's glory to renew in the church the riches of Christ's compassion and love for the divine will. In hope we call out:

We pray that the Spirit will rekindle in consumer societies a deeper love for lasting spiritual treasures. In hope we call out:

Presider: Loving God, your Spirit is the teacher of truth and leads us to the splendor of your glory. Like Christ, may we enflesh the beauty of Wisdom, for she is precious to our lasting good. Grant our prayer in Jesus' name.

Twenty-Eighth Sunday in Ordinary Time (C)

Presider: God desires that all people enjoy the freedom of the children of God. May the vitalizing Spirit of pentecost move us to proclaim to all peoples the truth of God's freeing love.

Petition Leader: Our response is, **"Jesus, descendant of David, hear us!"**

Naaman, the foreigner, experienced God's healing power through Elisha. May persons of other faith traditions experience God's healing love through the church's dedication to world peace. We pray:

Many Christians endure hardship and imprisonment for working to empower oppressed persons. May the Spirit be their strength in time of trial. We pray:

The Samaritan's encounter with Jesus brought wholeness. May the sacramental presence of Christ help restore wholeness to the sick and suffering. We pray:

Jesus affirmed the Samaritan's gratitude as an act of faith. May our faith express itself in our praise of God's goodness and lead to eternal glory. We pray:

Paul encouraged fidelity to Christ in every circumstance. May we bring the joy of the gospel to bear upon all aspects of our lives. We pray:

Many brothers and sisters have died with Christ. May they now live and reign with Christ (especially _____). We pray:

Presider: Redeeming God, your gift of faith leads to the fullness of life. For this we praise you and ask that our prayers be acceptable to you through Christ, our healer and Savior.

Twenty-Ninth Sunday in Ordinary Time (A)

Presider: Like the community of believers in Thessalonika, let us pray to be strong in hope and faithful in our labors of love.

Petition Leader: Our response today is, **"Lord, hear our prayer."**

For all who are followers of Christ; may the faith of the church manifest itself through fidelity to the gospel's call to conversion. We pray:

For all who are called to a ministry of teaching and preaching; may bishops and clergy, theologians and catechists perform their ministry in the power of the Holy Spirit. We pray:

For all who labor to free workplaces from harassment and exploitation; may this act of justice bear fruit for all employed in the workforce. We pray:

For good stewardship of our personal finances and resources; may we use our material blessings in keeping with gospel values. We pray:

For all who experience conflict between religious convictions and temporal values; may the Spirit uphold us in our commitment to God's truth. We pray:

For the sick and suffering among us; may the anointing Spirit bestow upon them the healing and peace of Christ. We pray:

Presider: God in heaven, there is no other beside you. Hear our prayers and help us to live in accord with the truth that sets us free in Christ, who lives and reigns forever.

Twenty-Ninth Sunday in Ordinary Time (B)

Presider: With confident faith let us call on the Savior's mercy that we may have God's help in every undertaking.

Petition Leader: Our prayer response today is, **"Christ Jesus, have mercy."**

May human aspirations for greatness be shaped by Christ's example, who became the servant of all, even to death on a cross. We humbly ask:

May persons in authority both in the church and in society exercise their roles with humility and care for the good of others. We humbly ask:

May parents and heads of household provide youth a witness to virtuous living, especially respect for personal integrity and spiritual values. We humbly ask:

May any who are plagued by self-hatred find in Christ the compassion and love of God that brings healing and peace. We humbly ask:

May the law of love free us from exploiting the goodwill and self-giving of others, particularly in marriage and families. We humbly ask:

May Christ, who gave his life as offering for sin, cleanse the dead of all iniquity and receive them into the reign of heaven (especially _____). We humbly ask:

Presider: Gracious God, in Christ you have revealed the immensity of your love for us. Accept our prayers and grant that your people may rejoice in the gift of your mercy through Christ, our mediator, who lives and reigns with you and the Holy Spirit forever.

Twenty-Ninth Sunday in Ordinary Time (C)

Presider: We are called to pray without ceasing. Let us call upon God's Spirit to help us persevere in prayer.

Petition Leader: Our prayer response is: **"Be with us, Holy Spirit."**

For all who are called to ministries of preaching and teaching in the church; may all bishops, theologians, homilists, and catechists be enriched by the gifts of the Spirit. We pray:

For persons who serve God's people as spiritual directors and retreat ministers; may their companionship bring spiritual refreshment to all who seek deeper intimacy with God. We pray:

For those who support the church through the ministry of prayer: contemplative women and men, retired clergy and religious, prayer associations, the elderly, and homebound; may their prayers continue to bring God's blessing to us. We pray:

For all whose hands are lifted up to God on behalf of the sick; may our voices be raised for those who cannot pray in time of trial. We pray:

For the Christian community gathered in prayer at the eucharistic table; may our praise and thanksgiving for God's goodness help us to grow spiritually. We pray:

For any who have lost hope in the power of intercessory prayer; may the Spirit renew the gift of prayer in persons who are spiritually discouraged. We pray:

Presider: God, our Guard and our Shade, sustain your Spirit in us that we may call upon you in time of trial and give you thanks in all our joys. Hear our prayers through Christ, our Lord.

Thirtieth Sunday in Ordinary Time (A)

Presider: Let us invoke the Spirit's grace that the gospel will echo forth in all our actions.

Petition Leader: Our prayer response is, **"Give us your love and grace, Lord."**

May these years of spiritual renewal in the church lead to deeper love for God. We ask in faith:

May our care for the needs and rights of immigrants witness to our love for neighbor. We ask in faith:

May personal profit not diminish our commitment to seek justice for the economically poor. We ask in faith:

May the prophetic counsel of the Spirit guide the church as it confronts the idols of consumer and power-driven societies. We ask in faith:

May the joy of the Spirit come to rest in our homes that they may be havens of love and affection. We ask in faith:

May all followers of Jesus be diligent in their efforts to eliminate sexual abuse in families and society. We ask in faith:

May respect for the well-being of others and for personal safety show itself in a firm commitment not to drive under the influence of alcohol or drugs. We ask in faith:

Presider: Compassionate God, give us your Spirit of love and grace that like Christ we may fulfill your law and come to eternal life in the reign of heaven. We ask this in Jesus' name.

Thirtieth Sunday in Ordinary Time (B)

Presider: Let us pray for the faith that gives new vision and life.

Petition Leader: Our prayer response is, **"Compassionate Healer, increase our faith."**

For all who seek to believe more deeply and love more generously, we call out to Christ and ask:

For persons who feel alienated from God's loving care and are spiritually discouraged, we call out to Christ and ask:

For believers who experience spiritual darkness and doubts on their journey, we call out to Christ and ask:

For physically disadvantaged and visually impaired persons who draw inner strength from their spiritual gifts, we call out to Christ and ask:

For the community of believers who celebrate God's reconciling love in word and sacrament, we call out to Christ and ask:

For persons whose lack of faith obstructs their vision of God's justice revealed in Jesus, we call out to Christ and ask:

Presider: Redeeming God, you have restored our fortunes in Christ. Console your people with a life-giving faith that we may join the great assembly that sings your praises in company with Christ forever.

Thirtieth Sunday in Ordinary Time (C)

Presider: Let us pray in solidarity with all who call on God's liberating love.

Petition Leader: Our prayer response is: **"God, hear our cry for help."**

Our God hears the cry of the oppressed. May our hearts take up the prayer of those seeking freedom from racial and sexual discrimination. We pray:

God has not turned from the wail of the orphan. May we reach out to young people who have not received healthy moral and spiritual guidance. We pray:

God is not indifferent to the needs of the widow. May we use our influence to secure justice for women and children left financially poor by the death of a spouse. We pray:

God stood by St. Paul when others abandoned him. May our support and friendship for others remain strong in their time of crisis and personal suffering. We pray:

God lifts up the lowly and fills them with good things. May the virtue of humility draw us closer to each other and to the heart of Christ. We pray:

God receives every plea for mercy. May those who have died trusting in God's compassion be freed from all distress (especially _____). We pray:

Presider: God in heaven, Jesus taught that whatever we do to the least among us we do to him. May our hearts be open to the cries of the poor so that our prayers will be heard by you, through Christ, our Savior.

Thirty-First Sunday in Ordinary Time (A)

Presider: Let us pray that the word of God will flourish in all believers.

Petition Leader: Our response today is, **"Creating God, hear our prayer."**

May our efforts to build vibrant communities of faith flow from our personal love for the word of God. We pray:

May those who hold teaching offices and ministries in the church light the way to intimacy with God and true love for neighbor. We pray:

May pastors and all pastoral ministers serve God's people with the gentleness and self-giving of loving fathers and mothers. We pray:

May the faithful receive the good news of salvation despite the human limitations of its ministers. We pray:

May Christian communities deepen their commitment to racial and gender equality out of love for the one God and Creator of all. We pray:

May our communion in the body and blood of Christ give us strength to live the mystery of Christ at home, at school, and in the workplace. We pray:

Presider: God our Creator, Father and Mother to us all, may we abide in love all the days of our life, thereby showing ourselves to be your sons and daughters. Grant our prayer in Jesus' name.

Thirty-First Sunday in Ordinary Time (B)

Presider: The eternal priesthood of Jesus Christ is a sign of God's favor for us. Let us pray through the mediation of God's anointed servant.

Petition Leader: Our response today is, **"God, hear us in Christ."**

Jesus took to heart the words of the covenant and has attained length of days in God's presence. May we take to heart the gospel of peace that leads to eternal life. We pray:

Jesus' self-offering birthed a new covenant of love that embraces all peoples. May God's grace inspire Christians to build inclusive communities of compassion. We pray:

Jesus absorbed himself in prayer and praise of God. May our love for God move us to be people of personal prayer and a community of praise. We pray:

Jesus showed that love for neighbor includes care for the least among us. May the Spirit help us discern the global dimensions of the gospel's love command. We pray:

Jesus reached out to persons kept marginal by religion and social custom. May the Spirit enable Christians to rise above alienating attitudes that eclipse God's mercy. We pray:

Jesus brought love's healing power to the sick and the sinner. May the anointing Spirit empower us to be a healing presence in our world. We pray:

Presider: God of our ancestors and Abba of Jesus, we have heard your word calling us to love you and our neighbor. Receive our prayers, and by the Spirit enable the Word of Life to take root in our lives. Grant this through Christ, our Eternal Priest.

Thirty-First Sunday in Ordinary Time (C)

Presider: Let us pray that God will bring the good in us to perfection.

Petition Leader: Our prayer response is, **"Loving God, hear our prayer."**

Mindful that God's Spirit is in all things, may we cultivate a deeper reverence for all creation, especially human life. We pray:

Remembering the power of prayer, may we call upon God's Spirit to guide us in all our ways. We pray:

Rejoicing that Christ came to bring all into the peace of God's household, may the church warmly embrace all that is beautiful and true in every culture. We pray:

Hearing that Zacchaeus sought to see Jesus, may we be inspired to search out Christ through a genuine love for sacred scripture. We pray:

Zacchaeus received Jesus into his home. May we welcome Christ in the person of the poor, the immigrant, and the spiritual seeker. We pray:

Believing that God's mercy reaches all flesh, may we be consoled in the hope that the dead receive new life in Christ (especially _____). We pray:

Presider: God of mercy, glorify Christ in us through our fidelity to your way of love. Receive our prayers and keep us in your loving care. We pray in Jesus' name.

Thirty-Second Sunday in Ordinary Time (A)

Presider: God's word calls us to love Wisdom. Let us pray that Wisdom's light will accompany us as we wait for Christ.

Petition Leader: Our prayer response is, **"Lord, send us your Spirit."**

We ask for the gift of sound judgment for our church and government leaders that their decisions may promote human flourishing. We call out in hope:

We invoke the Spirit to be with us in time of sorrow and long suffering that we may not lose heart in God's loving care. We call out in hope:

We implore the Spirit of God to accompany all who are approaching lifelong commitments, especially men and women religious, seminarians, and engaged couples. We call out in hope:

We ask that contemplative religious be blessed with the Spirit of holiness as they praise God from the rising to the setting of the sun. We call out in hope:

We pray that those dedicated to scientific and technological advancement will approach their tasks with prudence and respect for all creation. We call out in hope:

We entrust to the Spirit's grace our high school and college youth; may they be kept safe from all physical and spiritual harm. We call out in hope:

Presider: God of our ancestors, by your indwelling Spirit may your creation possess the gifts that enables it to be spiritually awake for Christ, in whose name we pray.

Thirty-Second Sunday in Ordinary Time (B)

Presider: In Christ we see the generosity of God's love and compassion. Let us pray to be filled with the same generous Spirit.

Petition Leader: Our prayer response today is, **"Enrich us with your Spirit."**

Christ died for the sake of the sinner; the Just One for the sake of the unjust. May our love receive the grateful and ungrateful repeatedly. We ask God:

In the midst of famine God sent blessing to the widow of Zarephath. May the church carry blessing to the world's hungry regardless of race or creed. We ask God:

Faced with certain death, the widow trusted the prophet's words and lived. May our faith trust the prophetic gospel of life in the midst of a culture of death. We ask God:

Jesus praised the widow's generosity. May her example inspire Christians to invest in the gospel from the substance of their lives. We ask God:

Jesus criticized leaders who devour the savings of the poor. May the church fearlessly denounce injustice that continues to exploit the economically poor. We ask God:

Christ's coming in glory will gather the just into the reign of heaven. May the dead who lived the gospel of compassion be clothed with the mantle of joy. We ask of God:

Presider: Consoling God, lavish your Spirit upon us that we may be transformed by the gospel and live as your holy people united with Christ, who appears before you on our behalf. We pray through Christ, our Lord.

Thirty-Second Sunday in Ordinary Time (C)

Presider: Confident of God's attentiveness to our pleading, let us raise our voices in joyful hope.

Petition Leader: Our prayer response is, **"Lord, hasten to help us."**

May God deliver us from terrorists and all who use violence as a means of coercion and vengeance. We pray:

May God guide us as we strive to remain committed to the gospel of peace in a discordant world. We pray:

May God protect our youth from the moral and spiritual deterioration of consumer and drug cultures. We pray:

May God's law of love rule over the hearts and minds of all in public office and positions of public responsibility. We pray:

May God console families who have lost a loved one through acts of violence and tragedy. We pray:

May God's faithful love be revealed to all who have died in the hope of eternal life (especially _____). We pray:

Presider: God, our refuge and strength, hear our prayers as we call upon your gracious love, through Christ, our Redeemer.

Thirty-Third Sunday in Ordinary Time (A)

Presider: Let us pray that our lives will yield a rich increase of love to God's glory, for our personal good and the well-being of others.

Petition Leader: Our prayer response today is, **"Loving God, hear our prayer."**

May the church be spiritually alert to the presence of Christ breaking into our world. We pray:

May the spiritual gifts of women, particularly wives and mothers, be a rich source of blessing to society and all households. We pray:

May the ministry of women who reach out to the poor and suffering ignite in others the fires of compassionate service. We pray:

May the legacies of love and faith bequeathed by our foremothers inspire us to leave behind a strong witness to gospel living. We pray:

May the Spirit help us to overcome any laziness and fear that hinders us from cultivating our God-given talents. We pray:

May we show ourselves to be faithful to Christ in the small matters of daily living that we may be found worthy of sharing the joy of Christ eternally. We pray:

Presider: God, giver of gifts, you call your servant church to bring forth a rich yield of faith, hope, and love. On the last day, may our works on behalf of your kingdom receive your praise at the gate of heaven. Grant our prayer in Jesus' name.

Thirty-Third Sunday in Ordinary Time (B)+

Presider: Let us pray for that wisdom which enables us to reflect the justice and holiness of God.

Petition Leader: Our prayer response today is, **"God, guide us by your Spirit."**

The dawning of God's reign is not without pain or distress. May the church be fortified by the Spirit of God as it labors for the enduring peace of heaven. In hope we call out:

God has promised a new creation more beautiful than the first. May the Spirit enlighten church and world leaders to discern its signs and cultivate its promises. In hope we call out:

We are called to hope in a new heaven and new earth. May we show ourselves to be responsible caretakers of this creation that we may find welcome in the one to come. In hope we call out:

[The following petition may be omitted after the year 2000.]
The new millennium has come as a time of hope. May we help prepare for a healthy future through our efforts to minimize all violence in the present. In hope we call out:

The Word assures us that creation will not pass until all the enemies of love come under the rule of Christ. May sincere believers not be distracted from the work of the gospel by predictions of the world's imminent end. In hope we call out:

The one sacrifice of Christ gathers us in the joy of one faith. May our sharing the one bread and one cup bring the Spirit to rest upon our community. In hope we call out:

Christ has delivered humanity from the powers of death. May the dead who have trusted God's saving power rise to eternal glory (especially _____). In hope we call out:

Presider: God, you guard our coming and our going. Keep your Spirit of wisdom alive in our hearts that we may dwell in the security of your love. Grant this in the name of Jesus.

+ An extra petition has been included here in anticipation of the new millennium. It is recommended that no more than six petitions be offered.

Thirty-Third Sunday in Ordinary Time (C)

Presider: In joyful hope of God's healing love, let us pray.

Petition Leader: Our response is, **"Christ, our Justice, hear us."**

For all who profess faith in God the Creator; may our lives respect the creation birthed with love and ordered to benefit all people. With hope we ask:

For the spiritual wisdom to read the signs of our times that call for spiritual maturity and moral integrity. With hope we ask:

For the ability to transform the earth through the principles of justice and care rather than to dominate it through greed, force, and destruction. With hope we ask:

For the grace to rise above personal laziness and to use our God-given talents and skills for personal sustenance and the common good. With hope we ask:

For the dignity of workers, particularly women; may employers and employees pursue together labor agreements that secure physical, moral, and spiritual well-being. With hope we ask:

For persons whose vision is restricted to earthly profit and power; may the Spirit kindle in them a love for their eternal destiny in the reign of heaven. With hope we ask:

Presider: God, our Creator, you have ordered all things to our benefit that we may praise you. Hear our prayers and help us to live in harmony with your Word Incarnate, Jesus Christ, who lives and reigns with you and the Holy Spirit, one God forever and ever.